THE
WIND-
FIRE
MOMENT

THE
WIND-
FIRE
MOMENT

BY JIM RUBSTELLO

ENGAGE
FAITH

ENGAGE FAITH PRESS • SEATTLE, WA

15 14 13 12 11   1 2 3 4

ISBN: 978-1-936672-04-2

For information, address

Engage Faith Press, PO Box 2222, Poulsbo WA 98370.

Scripture taken from the NEW AMERICAN
STANDARD BIBLE®, Copyright © 1960, 1962, 1963,
1968, 1971, 1972, 1973, 1975, 1977, 1995 by The Lockman
Foundation. Used by permission.

To receive The Wind-Fire Moment e-mails, please contact
jimmyrubtwfm@gmail.com.

Additional Wind-Fire Moments may be found at
http://thewindfiremoment.wordpress.com.

This book is dedicated to the heart. It allows us to live with genuine passion, even though it is constantly under attack. May the words in this book speak to strengthen, encourage, and heal those of courageous, downtrodden, or broken hearts.

Bob,

Thank you for taking the pictures at the party and for your kind words and suggestions on marketing the book.

I am glad that you have come to be a settling influence in Annie's life.

Reflecting His Glory,

Jim Restett

Psalm 46:10, II Cor 3:18

TABLE OF CONTENTS

FOREWORD....................................1

SPECIAL THANKS........................3

THE INTRO...............................7

THE PERSONAL TOUCH..............13

DAILY LIFE...............................39

EYES OF THE HEART..................71

THE JOURNEY..........................93

COMMUNITY............................119

KNOWING GOD........................135

THE HEART...............................161

THE FANTASTIC FOUR..............177

FOREWORD

I have always pictured these writings as a bit of Oswald Chambers meets Norman Rockwell. They are written about enjoying an intimate relationship with God, while experiencing it on the canvas of everyday life that people can relate to. These reflections have been inspired by the Holy Spirit, and I am sure that you will find that they often speak to situations that you are currently going through.

My heart is to often share inspiration that has come through the words of songs, Scriptures, quotes from movies, or things that God has opened my eyes to see. And to those, I add some of my thoughts that I hope will encourage you or inspire you to think outside the box. And maybe they'll even help you just to laugh a little.

The vision of this book is that it can be used by one person or in a gathering of many. It contains 52 Wind-Fire Moments, one for each week of the year, so it can be used as the point of a study for individual devotion or for a group. For a group study, I recommend taking one section and focusing on one Moment each week, for up to an eight-week study. Some people will simply use it as an icebreaker tool to help stimulate some discussion. There are always points of encouragement or challenges that will give you something to consider. I can also imagine churches using this book to help welcome new people or handing it out to those searching for God in tough times.

The book is divided into eight sections so that you can read straight through or look for inspiration on a specific theme. *The Personal Touch*, which has to be my favorite, is filled with stories of the people (and one very faithful dog) closest to me. *Knowing God* and *The Daily Life* will help bring the experience of an intimate relationship with God to a place that you can reach out and touch. The *Eyes of the Heart* section is meant to help you see God, while *The Heart* section will help you see yourself and others. *The Journey* is filled will heartfelt encouragements during some challenging times. *Community* is highlighted by a very unique concept that God put on my heart, called The Third Thursday Bistro, a place to find true fellowship. And finally, *The Fantastic Four* contains four Moments that generated overwhelming response from my readers as well as my emotions (and it has very little to do with superheroes). There will certainly be something for all to enjoy.

If you have purchased or been given this book, then know that with a humble heart, I am thankful and excited to be an *encourager* to you.

Reflecting His Glory,
Jim Rubstello

Special Thanks

To my mom, for being the one who asks the question, *Who encourages the encourager?* and then goes about encouraging in such wonderful ways. Thank you for always saying that you are proud of me, because it is what every little boy needs to hear his whole life. You have always been a rock of faith and support.

To my dad, who has always been there for me. I am so glad that we have gotten to experience so much together. You are an inspiration to me to always do better, and I am glad that I have been able to become a little more like you all the time.

To my wife, Dawn, twenty-eight years ago was "only the beginning," and I want you to know that I will always love you.

To Stephanie, Michael, and Katie, for allowing me to share parts of your lives with others, and for all of our great memories together that give my heart so much to look back on when finding inspiration. You all live lives of passion that are true to who you are, and that has always been something for me to find encouragement in watching.

To my friend Jim Rubart, I realize that a lot of what I do in sharing from the heart and encouraging the hearts of others, I had great fun in first discovering with you. You have been such a big part of getting this adventure started.

To Darci, for being the first one to suggest to me that I should start writing something on a weekly basis, and that maybe one day the writings could end up in a devotional.

To Pastor Steve Walker, for being the first of those receiving the Wind-Fire Moment e-mails to say that you could see my writings being published someday.

To Greg, Paul, and Andy, I am humbled by your tremendous generosity in stepping out to believe in the book and being willing to share it with others.

To John Eldredge, for having the words that began in *The Sacred Romance* to open the eyes of my heart to begin to fully understand that God is seeking an intimate relationship with me. And for that first *Wild at Heart* retreat in Colorado that started this journey by freeing my heart to be more alive to the Spirit so that I could be more aware of the hearts of others.

To all of the Wind-Fire Moment readers, who have been my support and the affirmation to the message of the Holy Spirit with your constant feedback. You are the reason that I have been able to continually write every week for nearly four years now. Thank you for traveling with me along this journey.

To the Third Thursday Bistro faithful, You are community, the way God intended it to be. Thank you so much for living out the Spirit of God in such a special way. You have made the Third Thursdays come to life, which has forever fueled my spirit with much hope and inspiration. **And to everyone who has ever visited** the Third Thursday Bistro and found just what you needed.

THE INTRO

The wind blows where it wishes, and you hear the sound of it, but you do not know where it comes from or where it is going, so is everyone who is born of the Spirit.

—John 3:8

It was October of 2001, and my good friend Jim (yes, his name is Jim also) and I were at a retreat in Colorado. That afternoon we were asked to take some free time and go talk with God. To ask Him, "God, who am I to You?" It may come in a name, we were told. *You are my Peter, my Joshua, my William Wallace, or my Maximus.* It may be in the context of a discipline. *You are Teacher. You are Encourager.*

I was not so sure about my mission. I mean, I could appreciate those that talked often about God communicating to them, but it was not my normal practice to speak to God and expect an answer right back. The speaker had even said, "It might not be something that is answered today." I was very interested in the answer, though, so I thought I would pursue it.

As I sat there wondering what God might say He thinks of me, my first thoughts were, "Well, Jim, you are actually a little disappointing. You don't stay consistent in your 'walk,' and though you do some good things, it is nothing that special."

I wasn't too excited to go out and listen to that. Then, I remembered that God has promised never to be condemning of us, and thus it must be Satan who was whispering this to me. In a moment of strength, I said, "Satan, I bind you in the power of Jesus Christ. You cannot have this time." The doubting thoughts disappeared, and I went out to find a spot on the side of a hill.

Sitting alone, some 9,000 feet above sea level, I had found my way to my own Mount Sinai. Now realize that the camp itself was already some 9,000 feet above sea level and that I had not gone on an amazing hike to get there. There was just some dirt, some rocks, some non-burning mountain vegetation, and me. I began to pray.

Having been encouraged to think of things that I was passionate about (to help know more of who I am), I began to tell God, "I love my wife. I love my kids. I love family. I love baseball. I love the sunrise and sunsets, the beach and the ocean." Suddenly, there was a big gust of wind that came through—the first wind I could remember since I had been at the retreat. "Yes, God, I do love the wind. And I love the power in a thunderstorm." I sat a little while longer, continuing to pray. Again, there was a gust of wind that came blowing across the hillside...

What is it about wind? It can *change the direction* of things. It can *bring quite a disruption* to situations. If you work with it, it can *make some things easier.* But, if you are working against it, then it might *increase the difficulty of your task.* And, as often as the wind can be known for its destructive, fear-inspiring power, it can also be a cool breeze that *brings relief, comfort, and peace.* This is why it is often used as a metaphor for the Holy Spirit.

It was through that same Holy Spirit that God spoke to me at that moment on that hill, saying, "You are to be my wind." God said, "I want you to go and make a difference. I want you to change what you can change, to disrupt what needs to be disrupted, to get people to hear my message, so that their life tasks may be easier. I want you to *encourage* and bring comfort and peace to those who are in need of that."

My reply to God was what it could only be, "OK, God, I will be Your wind." And with that, the wind stopped and did not come again. It was very quiet. I got up from where I was sitting and returned to the camp.

As I shared my story with those close to me over the next few days, God delivered to me affirmation through those people telling me, "That makes total sense for who you are." And when my friend Jim and I were on our way back to the Denver Airport, we both had thoughts that we would like to go and do some speaking about some of the messages we had just heard. I even said I would like to take that message to high school kids as well.

Now, I had never done any speaking before, so I am not sure why I thought this would be a good thing. But it seemed to be what God was telling us, and a few months later, Jim and I were doing the first of what became many men's retreats for some local churches. Just over a year later, I was standing (totally nervous) in front of the Bellevue Christian High School and Junior High chapels. That same year, I took on the ministry of coaching the high school baseball team. None of these things were sought after. They were all things that God presented.

All of this is to say: God has spoken to my heart and affirmed me through the encouraging words of others to put together weekly encouragements in e-mail. I had sent out my thoughts and stories to people before, and they had seemed to appreciate those thoughts, with one person even so bold as to say that I should do something every week.

Of course, my first response to this idea was that people don't want to be bothered every week, and what could I have to say that often. But I think that was the Enemy just trying to suffocate my heart. My heart comes alive when I get the opportunity to serve and encourage others. It's one of the reasons I also like to cook for other people so much, I guess.

That was the beginning of The Wind-Fire Moment. My occasional thoughts became a weekly e-mail of inspiration sent out to hundreds, now collected here in book form. I tell you my story here not only inform you of how this all began, but also to encourage you to ask God, "Who am I to You?" The answer can be life-changing...

THE
WIND-
FIRE
MOMENT

—SECTION ONE—

THE PERSONAL TOUCH

These eight writings are some of the closest to my heart, and I think they will speak to everyone. While they all focus on personal stories dealing with myself and my family, they include many situations where I hope that you will see yourself.

If you are a parent, you will definitely relate to many of these reflections through moments in time that you have witnessed yourself. If you are not a parent, you will probably remember having lived one of those moments yourself. And if you are person who loves animals, you might just shed a tear. There are stories of friendship and of encouraging, hopeful hearts, as well as stories that deal with life and death. In all of these, I pray you will find encouragement that will take you on a more intimate walk with God.

THE LEMONADE STAND

9/13/2007 AND 5/14/2009

You've all seen them: those little lemonade stands that pop up in your neighborhood. A table, a partially legible hand-written sign, some Dixie-cups filled with lukewarm lemonade (of varying strengths), and most importantly, a couple of eager-faced young kids who are experiencing for the first time the ups and downs of running a business in search of customers.

But *they believe*. They definitely believe that people will want to buy lemonade from them. I love the heart of a child!

My heart tugs every time that I see one of those stands. I know it is because I can remember when my daughter Stephanie, at age six, put up a lemonade stand at the end of our driveway. And I can still see the excitement in her face and the confidence that she was doing a great thing. The problem was, we lived in a cul-de-sac, way in the back of an obscure neighborhood. Friends got lost at least the first three times that they attempted to get to our house, and even family struggled if they hadn't been there for a while. Needless to say, potential customer traffic was limited.

So I always think back to that great unaffected hope and excitement that filled my daughter, but I also think of the hidden disappointment that must have come each time someone just passed by. Hers was a tender heart that was learning to take its first lumps.

That spring (and every spring since), I made a commitment to myself that I would stop every time that I saw a lemonade stand in my neighborhood. I would do my job of bringing that expected joy to the kids who were making that good old-fashioned effort. I would not be the one to deliver one of those lumps of disappointment.

I failed on my first opportunity to stay true to my new commitment. I was late somewhere and had some other excuse, I am sure. But I just drove right by a stand. I knew that I had fallen short. On the second go-round, I was off to watch a baseball game, came around a corner, and went quickly by a stand, with kids waving at me as I went by. I made it a couple of blocks and knew that it would bother me the whole night, so I turned around and took the long way back so that I could come at them in the same direction (I didn't want to make it obvious that I'd turned around). This was a full-service stand, with a box of snack bars as well as drinks. I bought lemonade and a snack bar and paid them a tip, which I told them was for the good effort of being out there. As I drove off, I called Stephanie, who was away at college. I had to tell my inspiration about my adventure.

I made one other stop that summer. As I pulled up to this particular stand and got out of my car, I met a man who was just leaving. I noticed as this guy got into his truck that his son was in the front seat with him. I think it takes a parent to make that stop. I'm sure he also knew what was going on inside the hearts of those kids.

Before he left, the man said, "These kids are doing quite a job, giving part of their proceeds to a cancer charity."

I found that at this stand, you could pay for one cup or pay a slightly higher, discounted price for two cups. I took one and paid for two. Again, I hoped to affirm in them that they were doing something great.

Just like that dad, who was intimately aware of the heart of a child, our Heavenly Father is intimately aware of the hearts of His children:

He knows the secrets of the heart.   —Psalm 44:21

He wants our hearts to be encouraged and alive.

This is also the passion of my heart. I begin each day by praying that God will present situations for me to be an encouragement to others. I pray that I will have the heart to recognize when those situations come up. I pray to make a difference. I do not have to seek them out, for they are abundant and all around. And they are for you, too.

My encouragement (or challenge, if you will) to you, then, is to **become a vessel that God uses to encourage the hearts of others.**

It will be up to you to find that lemonade stand in your life. Find a heart that can use some positive words. Find someone who is making an effort to accomplish something, and affirm that person. There is nothing like affirmation to help us know that we are on the right track with our efforts. Find people who appear down, and do something to pick them up. Maybe it is just doing something out of the blue for someone you don't know. The possibilities are endless. Need some specific ideas?

- Ask checkers at the grocery store how their day is going. Make the conversation be about them, even though you are the customer. You can see their countenance change.

- Thank someone for being a good friend, and tell that friend why he or she is a blessing to you.

- *Really listen* when someone talks to you, and go deeper into the conversation.

- Open a door for someone and smile.

- Make or buy some little treats and share them with others.

- Affirm people. Tell them, "You have what it takes," "You're doing a good job," "I appreciate you," or "You are beautiful." It works with all ages, too! You cannot do it enough.

Go and make a difference!

And if you are down and worn out right now, I pray that someone will bring you encouragement and affirmation. You might also be surprised, if you make the effort to encourage someone else, that you will find some new strength through that, too.

This was one of only two Wind-Fire Moments that I have sent out twice. The second time coincided with my daughter Stephanie graduating from college. Over the years, I have received more e-mails from people saying this is their favorite Moment than I have for any other. Most of those came from dads. This has become my "go-to" Moment when sharing with people what these writings are like.

Lone Girl Standing

10/28/2010

The rain had been coming down steadily for quite a while. The stadium lights shone down and lit the glistening turf. The referee's whistle blew that familiar cadence of three tweets to signify the end of the match. It was the end to the final game of the season for the two high school teams, and for my daughter Katie, like many of the other senior girls, it was the end of her final match. I knew that the whistle was coming, and as it sounded I stood and watched. Not only was it the end of some 12 years of watching my daughter play soccer, but it was the end of 18 years as a parent watching all three of my kids play sports. I watched as 20 of the 22 players on the field headed for the sidelines.

For some reason my daughter started jogging away from the sideline toward the far goal. At first I thought that for some reason she was going to retrieve one the extra game balls that was left by the goal, even though that was not her job.

But then I saw it. Standing motionless in the mouth of the goal was Lauren, the goalie. Lauren was not only a fellow senior who had just played her last game, but she was one of Katie's very good friends. Katie made it to the end of the field and the two of them embraced in what was obviously a very emotional moment for them both. Then they walked, together, over to their team.

I asked my daughter later if that was something that they had planned on doing for the end of the game, thinking that it would have been a cute plan. She said that it wasn't, that she had just seen her friend down there, not moving, and she had known what Lauren was feeling. Even better!

"So, I ran down to her," Katie said, "and when I got there, she had tears in her eyes, and then I broke down."

It was a very tender moment, especially to a parent who was already emotional from watching his daughter's last game. But I am afraid that the wonderful message that was spoken silently by Katie's gesture was missed by most everyone, whose focus was elsewhere.

Lone girl standing, but not left behind.

This was not a "rescue" in the sense that someone needed help. But it was, in the sense that someone needed someone who could be with her to get through the moment. And I want to use this moment to encourage us all.

We need to be a friend who will be aware of the moment. For Katie, this was her last game, and the whistle was the signal that it had come to the end. Most of us would be thinking about what the moment meant to us, not how others felt. And just like during the game, demonstrating her ability to always have a vision for the whole field, she was able to see what else was happening around her. She saw the lone girl standing.

The same holds true in our relationship with God: it is when we take our eyes off of ourselves that we can see so much more.

You shall love the Lord your God with all your heart, with all your soul, and with all your mind. This is the great and foremost commandment. The second is like it: **You shall love your neighbor as yourself.**

—Matthew 22:37–39

I find it interesting that Jesus talks little about loving our friends, besides that we should lay down our lives for them—which I guess covers that. But most of the time, he is talking of how we treat our neighbors, using the story of the Good Samaritan to tell us that everyone is our neighbor. So I must add the encouragement to you to be aware of the moment with your neighbor as well. It may be the greater challenge, but there may be no better way to show His love.

There are times that we just need someone to walk with us. Lauren did not need help walking off the field, but she needed someone to come alongside her, someone who knew just what she was feeling. She needed someone who would stop, give her a hug, and shed a tear with her. She did not need Katie to come and solve anything for her, but just to come and say, "I know." Do you understand the difference here? Sometimes when we are in need, we aren't always asking someone to spend time with us because we expect them to be able to solve anything. We are just hoping that they will come and sit with us, to make us laugh, or to listen to what we feel we have to say.

What kind of friend (neighbor) will you be? We should all be a friend like Katie, who can sense the moment and do the right thing. And we should all want to be a friend like Lauren, who lives in such a way that her friends will joyfully and selflessly meet her needs. Friendships like these are developed in community. When you are in high school, you are given that platform to live in, but after graduation, that community is not just given to you anymore. So, my encouragement goes out to all of us who don't live in high school anymore, those who have to work to find a community where actions like these exist. I think Katie and Lauren showed it is worth having.

Right now there is a rather large hole in my soul. I have no soccer match to look forward to. I have always loved watching Katie perform on the field of play; she scored her share of goals, always made the most beautiful passes, and handled the ball with some awesome moves. But I have come to realize that she saved her very best move on the field for after the final whistle. I wish I had had a camera to capture the moment, but I have a feeling it is a picture that I will never forget...

So many people have either already been the parent in this situation or can see this situation coming with their kids, that this reflection triggered a number of responses. I had a number of men respond by saying that it put tears into their eyes. The actions of those involved were wonderful lessons to share with others. As do all of the Moments in the Personal Touch section, this one always makes me very proud of the moment.

MAN'S BEST FRIEND

07/29/2010

For the first time in the 48-plus years of my life, I am without a family dog. And for the first time in 22 years, we do not have a dog that sleeps in our bedroom. You see, just the other day, I had to put our almost 14-year-old Golden Retriever, Isaiah, to sleep. Yes, he was living in "overtime" the last few years, but the reality of his absence has left a very big hole.

There are not many people who love dogs more than I do. And I love big dogs—the only reason that I do not have a polar bear for a pet is because it is not allowed. So I like to have large dogs that you can lie on the ground and give a big hug and a snuggle to. Isaiah weighed in the neighborhood of 85 pounds and looked like an over-sized middle linebacker. Some people might have said that he was "heavy."

Isaiah is the third dog that I have had to put to sleep, but this is the first time we did not also have a second dog to lessen the loss. And on top of that, I had to put Isaiah down in the midst of a 10-day stretch when my family was out of town. Man's best friend, who in his later years had to be everywhere I was, was nowhere to be found. Every time I wanted to make myself something to eat, I would think something like, "That sounds good; Isaiah will like some of that. Let's see, eight pizza rolls for me, and I'll cook two for Isa..." I was really alone.

(We do have three cats. And for all of you cat people, please take no offense. But cats cannot offer the constant and loyal companionship of a dog. They take too many timeouts to do what they want to do. OK, we do have one cat who has been trying to work on that problem in order to help me.)

The Wind-Fire Moment is a place to encourage you through the authentic thoughts from my heart that are inspired by the Spirit to share. I feel that I have been given grace to share with you, so I would like to encourage you by some of things that made Isaiah such a good companion. Here are some of Isaiah's attributes that would be good for us to take note of for ourselves:

He liked everyone he met. Isaiah was always happy to see people and very happy to meet someone new, and he always thought that new people should be happy to see him as well. When out on a walk, he wanted to go say "Hi" to anyone walking by, and he never had a problem with another dog. Even when the new people would only talk about what a beautiful dog that Shepherd-Husky was, failing to comment on Isaiah, he never took offense. He just stayed happy. He didn't have to "be the show." You had to love that about him.

He was very accepting of those who were different from him. He never had a problem with any of our cats and would always let them come and just lie around by him. The cats so enjoyed him that they picked up some dog mannerisms along the way. One of the cats had a habit of obnoxiously rubbing his face against Isaiah's face and trying to rub his nose in the dog's ear. Isaiah never snapped at the cat; he would just get up and move somewhere else. We should all be so accepting of others.

He always wanted to be near you. As I said earlier, Isaiah made every effort to know where you were, and though it was getting harder for him to get up and down, he still did it. You would let him know you were off to bed, and he would just stay lying there. But by the time you got under the covers, you would hear his nails come clacking across the wood floor, into the room. Then, after a slight hesitation, "Hmphff," and he was down for night. He didn't always have to be touching you, just in the vicinity. And if he felt like he needed a little attention, he would just roll over onto his back, stick that big belly up in the air, and start wagging his tail. How could I walk by that without stopping to give him a rub? He could be lying there half-asleep, and you would just lightly say his name, and the big tail would start thumping on the floor or against the wall. You had to love his passion for being with people.

He enjoyed his food. This made him a great companion of mine, since I love cooking for people and he loved to get his share of anything going on. He would just laser those sad retriever eyes at you, making sure you knew he was there for a purpose. He could hear the plastic bag that held the lunchmeat come out the refrigerator from two rooms away.

Yes, he did have his early life moments of stealing loaves of bread off the counter and running to get under the dining room table. The attempt to pry his jaws open to remove the bread was never easy.

Once, a guest was over and had a piece of carrot cake on a plate sitting on his lap while talking and watching TV. Isaiah thought that since it was accessible, the guest wanted to share. It was gone in an instant. I loved his passion for food.

On Isaiah's last day, he got up in the morning and went outside to lie on the front lawn. After quite a while, I called to see if he wanted to come in. He didn't move. I went over to him, and he struggled to open his eyes (later I would realize his face was swollen). I noticed that he had a little blood running out of his nose, so I got down on the ground next to him, but he seemed too tired to pick his head up. I went inside to call my wife, who was in Wyoming, but I could barely get a sentence out. "I think Isaiah... is going to... die today... and nobody is here." I called the vet and was able to make a time to take him in a few hours from then, and then I began what would be a couple hours of crying.

Over those few hours he picked his head up a couple of times and even got up and moved once. But his breathing seemed labored, and for the first time since I had known him, his tail did not wag. I lay down on the ground next to him and kept talking to him. I told him that he had lived a full and very good life and that if he was in pain, that it was really OK to just go to sleep and call it a life well done. But I believe what he was thinking was, "I would just rather stay out here on the lawn with you a little longer, my daddy."

I think I loved that the most about him.

I believe that I received more email responses from this reflection than from any other. It was amazing the number of people who actually were preparing to go through the steps of putting their dog to sleep, and how reading about it from me helped them to emotionally prepare. The Holy Spirit worked in very wonderful ways in knowing who needed to read this.

Reflecting Glory

11/29/2007

My life's "tagline" has become *Reflecting His Glory*. I sign most of my emails and cards, "Reflecting His Glory, Jim Rubstello." It is my reminder to be the one whom God created me to be, so that others will see His reflection shining off my life. To me, it is not a boast as much as it is a reminder of a goal.

Paul Colman wrote in his song "Sun-Stars-Moon,"

I want to be the moon, cause it reflects the sun
Don't want to be the star that shines on everyone.

Colman said that we were not made to be worshiped and that when we allow God to be the sole source of light and love, our soul finds its home. I like that!

But we all, with unveiled face beholding as in a mirror the glory of the Lord, are being transformed into the same image from glory to glory, just as from the Lord, the Spirit.   —2 Corinthians 3:18

This verse is the end of a passage where Paul was discussing that when Moses would come down from the mountain after having met with God, his face would be glowing. He would be reflecting God's glory. But he would then veil his face so that the others would not see this glow fading from his face. But that does not have to be the case with us.

For that which fades away was with glory, much more that which remains is in glory.   —2 Corinthians 3:11

The reflection never has to fade.

But the truth is, there are many of us who choose to walk around with veiled faces. When we do that, we are hiding our strengths and hiding the ability to be a reflection of God's glory. It is time to strip the veil away.

Why would we choose to live with that veil?

Sometimes we lack confidence in a situation. So we veil our strengths to avoid possible failure. Instead of stepping up to test that strength and show everyone what we have to offer, we choose not to act. We fear that we may not have enough within us to meet the challenge before us. We do not have what it takes to keep up with the others. So the Child of God becomes timid. This is not what God had in mind when He created us.

We feel that people may think of us as "too Christian." We hold back in standing up for things that are right, or acting in a way that would distinguish ourselves as living to a higher calling. This especially happens with young people not wanting to "weird out" their peer group. This even happens in the Christian schools, believe it or not. If a young person became comfortable in his or her God-given strengths, that person's peers might not be quite ready for that. So they decide it's just easier to hide their strength.

We are afraid to let others know who we really are and what we have to offer. There is something there that is holding us back. Look how long it took Aragorn (in the movie version of *The Lord of the Rings*) to acknowledge to others his true stature as King, and then to step into all of his strengths.

And worst of all, we wear a veil because we do not know who we are. We do not know whom it is that God created us to be, we do not know the strengths that He has created in us, and we have not yet asked Him to reveal them to us. We have yet to discover the instructions He has for us.

Think about Superman, if you will. He was one of the only superheroes to be born with his powers—just as we are born with our strengths. He didn't gain the ability to fly, X-ray vision, or super strength through a radioactive spider-bite or a chemical spill. He was born with those strengths. And it was his father who left him instructions on how to use his strengths, and to what purpose. This is just like us! We have a Heavenly Father who wants us to live out our strengths to achieve His purpose: *to reflect his glory!*

So I encourage those of you who have a veil over some part of your life: find the courage to raise your self-confidence and to go forth into that area you fear. Step up into boldness, and live a life that is distinguishable from the lives that are lived around you. Seek your Heavenly Father earnestly, asking Him to reveal to you your strengths and the purposes He has intended for you. And do not worry about what others will do or say to these efforts.

For you undoubtedly will find conflict on this journey. You will find some who try to hold you back because they have not yet found their strengths or don't even want to look. The road will be filled with obstacles because the enemy fears that you will find your strength. Sounds a bit like *Pilgrim's Progress*, doesn't it?

The late Brent Curtis, who co-authored *The Sacred Romance* with John Eldredge, said, *"Let people feel the weight of who you are... and let them deal with it."* My son and I have referenced this often as he has gone down the path of his life. It is my encouragement to all of you who would be hesitant for any reason to live as a reflection of the Father.

As I said, this is where my signature, "Reflecting His Glory," comes from. And if people would only gain one encouragement from me, I hope it would be encouragement to find their glory and live it out. It is putting aside a desire to have it be "all about me" and allowing God to show through.

I Am Sorry

10/29/2009

A couple of days ago, a young man named James, a fellow student and fraternity member at the college my son attends, took his own life with a gun. I don't really know how to process that, and I find myself wondering how I will walk my son, who has always been very sensitive to the matter of life and death, through this. Everyone will have questions, of course, but in a case like this, some of the answers may never be known. I know that I have said in the past that it is alright to not have an answer for everything, but it is still hard to accept not always knowing.

As I have tried to deal with this news, the only thing that keeps coming to me is **I'm sorry.**

 I am sorry that this happened to such a young person. I am sorry for this boy's family and what they will go through. And I am also sorry for my son, that he will now have to learn how to deal with this in his life.

The righteous cry and the Lord hears, and delivers them out of all their troubles. The Lord is near to the broken-hearted, and saves those that are crushed in spirit...

The Lord redeems the soul of his servants, and none of those who take refuge in Him will be condemned.   —Psalms 34: 17–18, 22

James, I don't know anything about why you felt you had to do what you did. I don't know what anyone said or did not say to you before this, or if you even reached out at all. I don't know if the body that you were born with was just not equipped or wired to handle what life here on earth was giving you. But my spirit is saddened, and I do want to say that **I am sorry...**

I am sorry for what didn't happen that might have made a difference.

I am sorry that your community was not able to save you, and even more sorry if you did not give them the chance to do so.

I am sorry if no one ever told you that being with you and helping you deal with your worst days would be so much better than not having you around.

I am sorry if anyone made the pressure of succeeding and becoming something too much for you to bear.

I am sorry if anyone ever told you that who you were, or what you were doing, was not good enough.

I am sorry if no one ever told you to find the things that make your heart come alive and then go do them.

I am sorry if no one ever told you that we *are all broken*, and that is why our Savior, who came to heal the broken-hearted, has to be such a real part of our lives, and that there is an intimate relationship with Him available here in this world.

I'm sorry if you never realized that God's arms are long and reaching to embrace you, and that in them is a place that we can all find rest.

I don't know how others who knew James handled this. Did they run to each other? Did they run to their families and hold them tight? Did they run to God and cry out, "Why?" I know that each member of our family got a text message from our son that said, "NEVER FORGET THAT I LOVE YOU VERY, VERY MUCH." And my response was to say, "It can never be said enough, my son. Your mother and I love you beyond the words that we can ever say."

Since you have in obedience to the truth purified your souls for a sincere love of the brethren, fervently love one another from the heart, for you have been born again not of the seed which is perishable, but the imperishable that is, through the living and enduring word of God.

—1 Peter 2:22–23

James, **I am sorry** if for some reason you did not know how much you were truly loved, not only by your family and your friends, but by the One who created you for relationship with Him.

My encouragement to everyone is to ask:

Is there something that you don't ever want **to be sorry** for not saying or doing?

Is there someone that you don't ever want **to be sorry** to for not reminding them how much you love them?

Sorry for not ever giving them a real hug to let them feel how much they really matter...

Sorry for not ever really listening to them...

Sorry for not encouraging them to find the joy and freedom of coming fully alive...

Sorry for not ever telling them that they have what it takes...

Sorry for never praying for that person to find the truth and intimacy of the gospel...

Sorry they never heard that in God's arms is a great place to find rest and that those arms are reaching out to them...

Now is as good a time as any to do those things. **Don't be sorry!**

This was a very hard reflection to write. I knew that there was great pain to be found in the young man's family, and I did not want to tread where I should not. But the Holy Spirit inspired me that there was encouragement and lesson for us all to be found here.

THE CHRISTMAS RECAP

12/27/2007

It is said, "It is better to give than to receive." When I moved into being married and having a family, I became a true believer in this. For years, I have gone into Christmas anticipating what my wife will think of her gifts and the joy on our kids faces when they get the unexpected. We have cherished family videos of each kid opening presents and shrieking in joy, often followed by dancing.

But what I want to tell you about here is the surprise I got from three presents given to me one year. Allow me to recap a little of that particular Christmas morning at the Rubstello house.

We had begun to move towards more of a "minimalist" Christmas, in the sense of how hard we worked on the Christmas pageantry. This year it was going to be about our time together, not the peripherals. Well, we got a puzzle finished, we watched *A Charlie Brown Christmas* (not to mention VeggieTales Christmas shows, the cartoon *Grinch*, and an evening of Jane Austen), we went as a family to the opening night of the movie *National Treasure 2*, we made cookies, we went out and looked at Christmas lights, we ate (and ate) some of our favorite meals, and my son started a new tradition of making Christmas Eve dessert: a blueberry cobbler that was enjoyed by all. We shared so very much together.

So when it came time for Christmas morning and the gifts, there was minimal anticipation on my part. Yes, I was anxious to see my wife open her gifts from me, as I am every year. But it was the gifts that my kids bought for me that turned out to be the highlight of my morning.

You see, I am one who likes to find out about another's heart and what stirs it to come alive. And I have always tried to get my kids to think in the same way, or I've at least hoped that they will find that desire as well. Well, all three of them were well in tune with that desire this particular Christmas.

From Stephanie (my oldest daughter): I have always wondered why my family never buys me a cookbook. I love to cook, and I am constantly on the lookout for new recipes to make for my family. I am always watching Giada De Laurentis on the Food Network, grabbing new ideas to try. I like Giada because her recipes do not require a lot of expensive, hard to find ingredients, and I can ad-lib with them, adding my own touches. Giada is my cooking mentor! (My mom is another.) Would not one of her cookbooks be a perfect gift for me?

Well, this Christmas brought me two Giada cookbooks, and my heart was very glad. Stephanie gave me one, and my wife bought the other one. These were great presents that I knew I would love to go through, and would have great fun with as I tried new dishes. My youngest (who loves pasta) grabbed the *Everyday Pasta* book, and said, "I need to find some recipes to request." Cooking them would be my pleasure.

From Michael (my son): I received a movie poster of *Dead Poets Society* to hang in my office. When I had my own office, the walls were decorated with a handful of movie posters that stirred my heart. Instead of having a business chart or an industry poster, I wanted people to know a bit about me. If you had entered there, you would have seen a beautiful print of Captain Jack Sparrow framed in wood that looked like an old treasure chest, as well as the posters for *Field of Dreams* (my favorite movie of all time), *Pride and Prejudice* (with Keira Knightly, a classic hopeless-romantic movie), and *Serendipity* (John Cusack, more romantic comedy for the romantic).

I had been wondering what movie poster should be next, but nothing stood out. *Dead Poets Society* was the perfect choice. Professor John Keating (played by Robin Williams) is my most inspiring movie character. The headline of the poster reads: "He was their inspiration. He made their lives extraordinary." Keating was a man who had a passion to bring the hearts of others alive, and he strived to get them to think outside the box. This is who I want to be; this is what I want to do.

From Katie (my youngest): In a frame, written on a piece of school note-book paper, was a list titled "Dad's Weekday Highlights." It listed each day (each day was a word cut from a magazine) with its particular schedule, though the days were all quite similar.

Each day started with *Make Katie's sandwich/Drive her to school*, followed by *Daily Schnoz*, which is a segment on the local sports radio that I would turn to during our morning drives to school. It always opened with a sound-bite from a Frank Sinatra song, and then went to interviews with other sports broadcasters around the country. Katie likes hearing the different accents of the people from around the country (Wednesday's variation: *This is donut day.*)

Next on the list is *Work* (Thursday's variation: *Get Wind-Fire Moment out*), then *Watch Friends/Make dinner.* (Friday's variation: *Dinner out?*) My family has become obsessed with the show *Friends*, and my wife likes to have it on for her down time when she gets home from teaching. Every other Tuesday the schedule reads *Men's Bible Study*.

And each night ends with my (our) favorite TV shows to watch. Often, I watch them with Katie. The funny thing is that she correctly lists which nights to DVR a show (with the viewing time listed on another night) and which nights that we have to choose what to watch at a certain time.

The point here is, only a third-born (baby of the family) would list out a very repetitive week like this—one that greatly involves her—and call it "Dad's Weekday Highlights." But only a third-born (baby of the family) knows that they truly *are* my weekly highlights. My eyes filled with tears as I read "my" schedule.

What is my point of encouragement to you by sharing these gifts that I received? I don't really know. Maybe it is to encourage you to think about giving gifts that will stir someone's heart, whether it be for Christmas, Valentine's Day, Birthdays, Anniversaries, Graduations, and other special days throughout the year. Maybe it is to encourage you to choose to live a life with the passion of Professor John Keating and inspire others to let their hearts come alive. Maybe it is just to tell you how my heart was filled with great joy by some very special little things, so that you will remember to find great joy in the little things as well. Maybe it is just to encourage you to have your heart on alert, to recognize when these moments come.

You choose...

I cannot believe how time has flown by, that this Christmas was back in 2007. I still hope that this reflection will help you strive to see what really stirs the heart of others, and that you may think of gifts that will uniquely accomplish that. I enjoyed reading the responses to this Moment, hearing the stories from others about what they have done.

MORE THAN A STORY

03/20/2008 AND 04/01/2010

It was a Friday afternoon in April, and my wife, Dawn, and I were standing in a cemetery on a hillside just west of Portland, Oregon. We stood there, surrounded by her dad's brothers and sisters, who had all flown in to attend the funeral of their brother, who had just passed away from cancer.

What a week it had been. Dawn's dad passed away early on Tuesday morning. He had asked to be buried in a particular small cemetery on a hillside near Beaverton, Oregon. Dawn had just two days to arrange for the body to be taken care of and transported to the Portland area (a three-hour trip), and we had no one to perform a service. Dawn wanted someone who could deliver a good Christian message to her dad's family of unbelievers, so I reached out to a man I had met in my industry, who I knew was strong in his faith. I asked him if he could do us a favor and find a pastor who would be willing do a service in a couple days for some people he had never met. To make it an even bigger favor, the service was going to be on Good Friday.

We met the pastor on Friday, right before the service. I had spoken to him on the phone the day before to give him some background on my father-in-law and the circumstances surrounding his death.

My father-in-law, Dale, often entertained us with his opinionated and headstrong personality (some of that may have passed to his daughter). Christianity was not something he was going to buy into. If there was a heaven, he was a good enough person that he should get in—no need to be part of the group of hypocrites that he saw at church every week. In the fall, when his cancer was announced to be incurable, giving him only four to six months to live, it was very hard on Dawn to know that he had not made a decision to secure his salvation. We began diligently praying. And then, four months later, totally out of the blue, he announced to Dawn that he had become a Christian. A pastor that we did not even know had been coming by to visit him, and through their talks, Dale had heard a particular message: the message that only perfection will get us into heaven to be with God, and that no matter how good we are, no one is perfect. It takes God seeing us through His Son, Jesus Christ, to see us as perfect. That was good enough for Dale.

In that little hillside cemetery, the pastor began the service. "Here we are on a hillside, just outside of town, at approximately 2:30 in the afternoon. It was almost 2000 years ago, on a hillside just like this, at about 2:30 in the afternoon, that Jesus Christ hung on the cross and said, 'It is finished.' And we are here on what is now called Good Friday. But I am here to tell you that it is not a Good Friday. Today, it is a Great Friday! For what many of you might not know, is that a little more than a month ago, Dale gave his life to the Lord. . ."

The day Dawn found out about her dad's decision she went to school to pick up our kids and tell them of their grandfather's "life decision." Michael, then in first grade, ran, with child-like exuberance, to tell other parents who were standing around. "My grandpa accepted Jesus!" The next morning at the school's teacher devotion time, Stephanie's third-grade teacher just had to share the story of how her student had for months prayed every day in class for her grandfather to be saved, and how inspired she, the teacher, was by having been witness to that dedicated faith of a caring child, and then to see it rewarded in victory of salvation.

As the pastor finished the service that day, he said, "Though Jesus Christ said that day on the cross, 'It is finished,' today we celebrate that for Dale Ornduff, it is not finished, but only beginning!"

Easter would never be the same for me!

We drove back home that night. The next morning there would be another service for those in our local area, this time performed by the pastor who had brought Dale to the Lord. I am not sure if we even went to church on Easter Sunday, for the Easter message of new life and restoration could not be shared any clearer than what we had just lived over the last week.

So, let me encourage you the next time that you get ready to celebrate Easter, let it begin with a Great Friday! Remember the message that His death, and the following resurrection and restoration, is what it took to bring Life: Life that is eternal, and that has already started for all who will choose to believe. Take time to know that it took God moving heaven and earth to conquer sin and to restore us to the glory that God had intended for his children...

I also know that it took God and the prayers of many, including the tireless faith of little children, to bring together this story: finding a pastor dedicated to visiting a near-stranger week after week, moving a very stubborn heart, helping Dawn make arrangements for an out-of-town funeral in just two days, and finding a way to bring joy to the hearts of a daughter, son-in-law, and grandchildren who were losing someone so close to them.

It took a death to deliver a message of a new beginning.

I grew up in Sunday school, I memorized the Golden Rule
And how Jesus came to set the sinner free
I know the story inside out; I can tell you all about
The path that led Him up to Calvary
But ask me why He loves me, and I don't know what to say
But I'll never be the same
Because He changed my life when He became
Everything to me, He's more than a story,
More than words on a page of history
He's the air that I breathe
The water I thirst for
The ground beneath my feet, He's everything
   —"Everything to Me" by Avalon

This Moment spoke to many different people on all kinds of levels, and it continues to speak to me. It is the second reflection that I have repeated, and I have been told that I could use it every year and people would not get tired of the reminder. I could think of no better way to end this section than the personal story that has impacted our lives the most deeply.

—SECTION TWO—

DAILY LIFE

These ten writings are possibly the best demonstrations of why I try to describe *The Wind-Fire Moment* as having a little Norman Rockwell. I put these under the title of Daily Life, as they are all images of seeing God and His work in our everyday walk.

The inspirations came from all around and from all ages. I love these stories, and I think you will love many of them as well.

CHOOSE YOUR GROUND

9/11/2008

This is the time of year when students are going back to school, and the Spirit recently drew me to the parable of the Sower and the seeds. I see this as a very important message to young people. I used this message once with a group of my senior baseball players as a prep talk for college, and I wish to this day that I had carried that on as a tradition. The parable talks about seeds being scattered by the Sower, but the message I want to give you here is that we choose our ground.

To that point, I want to use this as an encouragement to all of you, since we will find ourselves, at any age, choosing the ground upon which we will settle in for our spiritual growth. I hope it reaches out especially to those of you who are parents or spend time leading or mentoring young people.

We should all be fairly familiar with this parable found in Matthew 13, Mark 4, and Luke 8, but here is a little refresher:

The kingdom of heaven may be compared to a man who sowed good seed in his field, and as he sowed, the seed fell in different places:

1. Some seeds fell beside the road, and the birds came and ate them up.

2. Others fell upon the rocky places where they did not have much soil, and they immediately sprang up. But because they had no depth of soil, when the sun rose, they were scorched, and because they had no root, they withered away.

3. Others fell among the thorns, and the thorns came up and choked them out.

4. And others fell on the good soil and yielded a crop, some a hundredfold, some sixty, and some thirty.

Jesus was talking about what happens to the Word when it lands upon different types of people. And I would like to relate that to what can happen to the those with a "good heart" when they put themselves on varying types of soil. I want to emphasize that we often get a choice of what kind of soil to surround ourselves with.

A reminder about what happens when the good seed...

Falls beside the road: *"then the devil comes and takes away the word from their heart, so that they may not believe and be saved."* —Mark 4:15

This means it never got to the field at all. Regardless of rocks, thorns, or good soil, these seeds just aimlessly landed. Whether it is from carelessness, lack of planning, or just by chance, it leads to a quick spiritual death when you settle in a place where your roots cannot begin to grow at all.

Falls into the rocky soil: *"those who, when they hear, receive the word with joy: and they have no firm root in themselves, but are only temporary: then when affliction and persecution arises because of the word (or in a time of temptation), immediately they fall away."* —verses 16 and 17

How often do we see those joyful young believers who stand ready to face the world? Here they have hit soil and have started to grow, but when they have chosen a ground that does not provide nourishment for stability and substance to their faith, they are taken out quickly. It is still ground that does have in its nature the conditions to grow firm in one's faith, but there are obstacles here that are maybe not so apparent as the ones by the road.

Falls among the thorns: *"this is the man who has heard the word: and the worries of the world, and the deceitfulness of riches, and the desires of other things enter in, and choke the word, and it becomes unfruitful."* —verses 18 and 19

Again, these people have every intention of bearing the fruit of the Spirit, but the world is allowed to take over. There is growth, but there is the deception of living among the thorns. Think of a garden for a minute. If the garden has plants that have thorns, the ones with the biggest thorns often have showy flowers to entice us. And those with small thorns quickly entangle themselves throughout everything without even being noticed. Before you know it, the Word is choked out, and it is harder for caring people to come in and reach the spirit inside.

Falls among the good soil: *"these are the one who have heard the word in an honest and good heart, and hold it fast, and bear fruit with perseverance."* —verse 20

It is the "honest and good heart" that does what is necessary to go to fertile ground, and it will be able to hold fast and bear fruit. This person chooses the right people to be around and the right activities to be a part of. Then, when the deceitfulness of the world comes knocking, they are able to follow the calling of Micah 6:8, *"to do justice, to love kindness (mercy), and to walk humbly with your God."*

Before I leave the good soil, I want to clarify that this does not mean that you must choose to go only where it is safe, where the ground is being tilled and fertilized for you. How then would any of us, young or old, be able to reach out and make a difference in the lives of others? How would we go into mission fields?

I think of young people going to college. Sure, a Christian college is a more fertile ground, much less likely to choke out the Word. But that does not mean that those with honest and good hearts cannot go to another college and "hold it fast, and bear fruit with perseverance." This is good seed that we are talking about here! The students would just need to be fully aware to maintain the ground that they have chosen to settle in.

What does this all mean, in real life terms, to choose your ground? For young people, it can mean choosing what group of friends they will commit their time to, or what activities that they will allow themselves to partake in or even be around. Will the life around them begin to choke out the Word in their spiritual life?

For all of us, will we let the deceitfulness of riches or the worries of the world come and choke out the Spirit inside us? Have we spent enough time in fellowship, in the Word, and in relationship with the Father to have given ourselves enough depth in our faith that we do not end up temporary in our stance on what we believe? Or will we just fall away or quickly be taken out by the enemy?

These are important questions to be thinking of. I encourage you to challenge not only yourselves with this, but to challenge those around you and whom you love as well.

Choose your ground!

I have a great passion for young people, and having spent seven years as a high school coach, I was able to see how important it was for the youth to choose the right situations and places to put themselves into. And it continues on for all of us at any age. This message resonated with many parents, and I hope it will encourage any of you who have those choices to make.

SEEKING GREAT JOY

05/07/2009

How many colors are in a rainbow? Did you know that there are seven? I wonder if you can name them and the order in which they appear. But my real question is: How many of those seven colors do you usually see when you glance at a rainbow? I know that you have never thought about it, especially since most of us thought there were only five to begin with. I mean, that's how many colors are in a Lifesavers pack of assorted flavors, and that looks like a rainbow to me. Just do me a favor the next time that you see a rainbow: try and count the colors—unless you're driving and might crash. More on this later...

Years ago, I wrote a Wind-Fire Moment about a prayer request that I made in my men's group, that I would like "great joy." I went about watching and looking for it that week and wrote about what I found.

Here it is a year and a half later, and I found myself praying this again. I had opened a journal of mine that I have used for talking to God, which I had not opened in two years. I found myself thinking one morning, "What is it that I should be praying for?" The answer came quickly: "Great joy, and a heart to see the needs of others." The answers to my prayer came fast and furious:

1. As I was driving to my favorite donut place, I made the pointed effort to come to a stop at a crosswalk where a dad and a young daughter were waiting. As they crossed, the little girl looked at me, and I smiled. She waved and returned a precious smile of her own. Normally, I would have been busy playing with my phone or waiting impatiently for them to hurry across. But this morning, I took the time to look, and it was great joy to my heart.

2. When I made it to the donut shop, the lady inside wanted to know where my daughter was. (Getting donuts together had been our weekly tradition, but now that my daughter has a license, we don't get to share the drive to school

in the mornings.) As we continued to chat about our kids, she told me about a struggle with her youngest. We had a nice talk, and I realized that God had prepared my heart to hear this woman share her frustrations.

3. In the mail that day at work, I received a surprise package with a DVD and book. The week before, I had entertained a gentleman who works for Rick Steves, whose travel show we regularly watch at our house. I had mentioned that we'd just watched the show on Provence, France, and had really enjoyed it. Next thing you know, he sent me an eight-episode DVD of France and a book. It was completely unexpected and something my wife was thrilled that I got: great, unexpected joy.

I compiled a long list of things of great joy over the following days, but I won't bore you with them all. What I want to encourage you with is that these moments of joy came when I was praying and looking for them. But then, after two days, I quit praying. I got busy and didn't even think to look for joy, and it did not come. So I started praying and watching again.

4. I got to work one day and found an e-mail from my daughter containing two songs she had written, looking for me to give her some feedback. We had some nice sharing back and forth. It made my heart feel good and it was great joy.

5. Getting back to that rainbow: I was driving home one night and saw a rainbow in the distance. It was cool to see the end of it hitting off Lake Washington. But as I drove farther the rainbow seem to jump closer, and I could see vivid colors. I saw Red, Orange, Yellow, and Green, and though I cannot say I saw Blue, Indigo, and Purple distinctly, I saw two of them. I had never seen such color! It was incredible; it was great joy.

To find joy, you must first seek it, and I encourage you to give it a try, to pray to God that your eyes and heart are open to recognize when it is being offered. And I encourage you to do it daily, because we miss out on so much when we do not take the time to seek out great joy or ready our hearts to receive it.

I will end by sharing with you a day of great joy that God delivered to me a couple of years ago, because it so charged my heart that I am still finding great joy in reminiscing about the day. Read enough of *The Wind-Fire Moment*, and you will know about my passions for being inspired by music and for cooking for others. Well, God obviously knows this as well.

A local church hosted a concert with the bands Third Day, Brandon Heath, and an Australian group named Revive. Through a friend, we found a way to invite them all out to our winery house, where I made them lunch. Twenty people showed up, and they all sat at one long table. It looked like the feast in heaven. The bands were two days from finishing their tour and said this was the first time that they had gotten a chance to all gather together somewhere.

My daughter and one of her friends helped serve. Their eyes were so big all day long! I think it was great joy for them as well. A couple of other special friends also joined in to help be of service. It was a wonderful afternoon of fellowship.

And in such a cool gesture, Mac Powell (lead singer of Third Day) asked if he could get five minutes of my time so that he could hear my story. How cool is that—to reach out to someone you have just met and truly want to hear that person's story. I want to have that kind of heart!

I share this because it was such a wonderful gift that God chose to deliver to this heart that has been through some major struggles. I had prayed that God would have this day completely. God gave my heart great joy to do the things that make it come alive (cooking and hospitality) and to be able to minister back to those who have ministered so much to me.

Thank you, Lord, for You are faithful and true! And I pray that you, my reader, will *seek and find* great joy!

I believe that it is important for us to look and see where God is delivering great joy to us even in the simplest of places. And while the last story may feel a bit like bragging, it was such a day of great joy in a way that only God could deliver that I just had to share it with you. I have taken to heart the gesture from Mac Powell in asking to hear my story and begun to ask that of others. I believe that it has been a blessing to those who have gotten to share, and I know it has blessed my life each time; I would encourage you to make this a practice as well.

SENSES

06/05/2008

The Lord is my Shepherd, I shall not want
He makes me lie down in green pastures
He leads me beside still waters
He restores my soul...

    —Psalm 23:1–3a

Psalm 23 has been put on posters, written about in books, turned into songs, and memorized by many. But I think what we often hear is, "The Lord is my Shepherd, I shall not want... yada, yada, yada..." and then we don't take notice again until, "Even though I walk through the valley of the shadow of death..." followed by fearing no evil, the comfort from the rod and staff, etc. But, if we do that, we miss something very important to our walk with God:

He makes me lie down in green pastures! He leads me beside still waters! Why do we gloss over this critical piece to our survival? Is it because the words aren't inspiring in sound or vision? I want to encourage you to see what God is imploring you to do here. He wants you to *stop* for a while and to *be still*. In this way, you can best seek His face. And what does this direction lead us to—a restored soul!

I have discovered a couple of very essential things to my survival of late, based on the theory that if you lose one of your senses, your other senses become heightened over time.

The other week I was sitting in our living room with the windows open. Because it was quiet, I was able to hear the sound of the first raindrops pounding on the leaves of the hosta plants outside. So I went and sat right in front of the window, turned my back to the window, and shut my eyes.

My theory is, if I can hear myself breathing, then I have blocked out enough of everything else in my thoughts that I am open to receive inspiration from the Spirit. With my eyes closed, I heard the rain, I heard the sound of birds all over the neighborhood, squirrels chattering in the trees, some noises from the house, and someone moving around upstairs. The aroma of the coffee I was holding made it to my nose. Then after just listening to the quiet and letting God talk to me about things heavy on my heart and about new hope, I turned around to face the window and opened my eyes. It was amazing how the color of the trees stood out and the branches seemed to hold such detail—all because I stopped to be still, to listen.

> *When my heart is overwhelmed and the well has all run dry*
> *When I'm dwelling on myself, or the mountains I must climb*
> *When I sense the desert storms, blowing deep inside*
> *I know in Your arms there's rest, and in Your hands there's life*
>
> *Take me to a quiet place, where I can taste a little bit of heaven*
> *Take me to a quiet place, where I can know the wonders of your love*
> *Lay me down in fields of grace, where I may seek your face*
> *In a quiet place*
>
> *When the sounds of city noise, drown the voice I long to hear*
> *When the peace that gives me joy, has seemed to disappear*
> *There's a whisper in the silence, that's drawing me near*
>
> *Where all I long to hear, is Your tranquil, still small voice*
> *And where all my anxious fears are replaced with Your joy*
> *Take me to a quiet place...*

—"A Quiet Place" by Dave Irish

Oh, the sadness of how we all let the sounds of city noise drown out the voice we long to hear! We never stop to just to lie down in the pastures or to sit by still waters. We just keep going, and we just keep filling our lives with things.

My daughter Katie is the best person I know at realizing that she needs her downtime. This is usually accomplished by heading into our garage and skating around and around. Or she heads to a couch or to her bed to do some writing.

She quit her select soccer team after five years, right after they had just climbed back to be one of the eight best teams in the state for their age, because, with all the things that she needs and wants to do, it was taking too much commitment and time. It was taking away the peace that gives her joy. She needed to make sure that her soul could be restored. What a mature decision she made.

My encouragement to you is to take heed. See that God wants to *make* you lie down in the fields and smell the flowers. See that God wants to *lead* you to still waters. *He wants you to seek His face so that He can restore your soul!* The best thing about it is that there is no pressure on you to perform, when you just sit and listen.

Listen to yourself breathing. And then you might be surprised Who else you hear...

This message definitely hit home with those who take some of that time to be in quiet. I received many emails telling me of what others had heard recently during their times alone with God. I hope that I was able to paint that picture for you so that if you are not in the habit of taking some time out for this, that you will consider it.

Want vs. Seek

05/29/2008

My daughter and I went to see one of our favorite speakers come talk at a local church about "walking with God." It was a very good evening, and I was not disappointed in my expectation that his message, and his engaging way of speaking, would hit home and connect with my 15-year-old. His message is practical for any age, and I knew she would enjoy him. Afterwards, we joined my friend Jim and his 15-year-old son for dinner at Red Robin to unpack the evening. I really wanted to hear what spoke to the hearts of 15-year-olds, and I wanted them to be able to hear from each other how the message impacted their spiritual lives.

Both of them had some really cool things to say that showed how in touch they were with their own spiritual lives and that showed they knew just what they needed to enrich those lives. Then, Jim's son said something about his struggle to consistently walk with God that I took notice of. His words were, "I want it more than I seek it."

I _want_ that intimate walking with God more than I _seek_ it.

Do you see the amazing honesty in that statement? I think that if I could get all of us to speak honestly, we would find that this is how we approach many things in our lives. Take this topic of intimately walking with God. I do not know why any of us would not want that, but it takes the act of seeking for it to become a part of who we are. The fact is that taking time for intimacy with God seems to get lost in our busy schedules and our misguided prioritizing.

O God, Thou art my God; I shall _seek_ Thee earnestly. My soul thirsts for thee, my flesh yearns for Thee, in a dry and weary land where there is no water.   —Psalm 64:1

Don't you just like saying, "O God, Thou art my God; I seek Thee earnestly"? I like the way that it fires up my soul.

It is no secret that we all struggle with our sinful nature. I have seen good Christian people struggle with long-time sin in a particular area of life. They truly want to get rid of it, and each time I see them they are ready to tell me of their struggle and the desire to be set free. But then I come to realize that they are not really seeking that freedom, just getting some false healing from talking about their desire to change.

And my people who are called by My name humble themselves and pray, and <u>seek</u> My face and turn from their wicked ways, then I will hear from heaven and I will forgive their sin, and will heal their land.
—2 Chronicles 7:14

Depart from evil and do good. <u>Seek</u> peace and pursue it.
—Psalm 34:14

My encouragement to you here is to be ready to take action! Be ready the next time that you get to that place in your spiritual life where the Spirit touches your heart and your heart speaks from deep within. Your heart will speak the things it desires, or speak to the areas of your life that need some adjusting. Then you must follow that right up with what should be the first step of action: seek and pursue it.

But <u>seek</u> first His kingdom and His righteousness...
—Matthew 6:33

How many things outside of our spiritual life do we approach in the same way? We *want* to lose some weight and get in better shape. But do we *seek* after that which will bring about change? We *want* to do better at controlling our spending habits, to improve our time management, to spend more time focusing on our families, but often we find ourselves in the same place, still *wanting*. Why?

Because we have failed to really seek out change in how we are living. We lack the passion that is needed to break free from the chains that are binding us. It is that same passion that can be read in all of these scriptures that are telling us to seek.

Ask, and it shall be given to you; <u>seek</u> and you shall find; knock and it shall be opened to you. —Matthew 7:7

The answer is clear! It is time to *seek*! It is not the time to stand in place and expect it all to change around you. Seek out those things that you have discovered to be the treasures of your heart...

...for where your treasure is, there will your heart be also.
—Matthew 6:21

Seek to improve your intimate walking with God. Seek Him on a daily basis, not just when you are at the end of your rope. And do not just seek Him out as a request line, but sit in the still and the quiet so that you can just listen to Him. Seek to live out the glory that He has purposed for your life. Seek out the blessings that He has for you, and pass along your gifts into the lives others. What are you filling up your time with that is more important than this?

If you have been raised up with Christ, keep <u>seeking</u> the things above.
—Colossians 3:1

I pray that you will all have the desire to *seek* that will be equal to your desire of want.

Many people responded to this by saying that they often find that they too have more want than seek in them, and that this was a strong reminder to them to make the effort to seek.

BEING AUTHENTIC

02/26/2009

So, how goes your battle? I hope that you are finding victories and joy. How is your heart doing? Is it flourishing and alive with passion, or is it a little beaten down and weary? Or worse, is it functional but just idling in some middle ground? I would really like to know—really.

I know that I am writing this to a lot of people. When first written as a weekly email, *The Wind-Fire Moment* went to some people that I saw and communicated with often, to some I didn't, and to some I had never met. But my heart truly desires to know how you all are doing, and I pray that you are doing well. Really!

In each reflection I open myself up in an attempt to be authentic. I know it may sound strange, but from the depth of my soul, I want you to know that someone really cares how your heart is. That is how I would like to encourage you: by letting you know that I am concerned about how you are doing. It is that plain and simple.

Let me also encourage you to be authentic. Authenticity is one of my core values, and I believe it is something that is missing from too many of us and, I'm afraid, from many churches.

I am not here to tell you the secrets to the "7 Steps to Authentic Christianity" or set up for you the "30 Days to An Authentic Driven Life," but I would like to share a couple of things to encourage you in adding more authenticity to your daily lives.

By definition, authentic means: not false or copied; genuine; real

My encouragement is to be yourself. Don't try to be the "happy-go-lucky Christian" if that is not where your heart is at. We do not need to be on stage for anyone. This is not being authentic. I definitely believe that Jesus never decided, when He was going to walk to Jerusalem for the weekend, that "I need to put on my happy face." There is no reason to pretend that everything is peachy if it is not. I am not saying you need to spread ashes on your forehead and tear your clothes, lamenting "woe is me" either. But being authentic is feeling free to let people know the times when you are worn down, when you are struggling, and when you have questions.

You are no less of a person if you admit to life being hard for you. Your Christianity is not tainted if you share real struggles with others. In fact, it is more real. It is more authentic. (But note: being authentic does not mean constantly baring your soul or constantly drowning people with your struggles.)

Authenticity also means that you can say what you actually mean to say, and then follow that up by living accordingly to your words. It can mean risking that you might ruffle the feathers of a friend (if you have earned the right) with an observation, but then it also means being open to hearing something about yourself as well. It means that you open your heart to share what your dreams and passions are, so that others can see the genuine you. If everyone would do this, it would be so refreshing.

Authentic is also defined as: origin supported by unquestionable evidence

A Jim Rubstello translation: be like Jesus. Your origin is your Creator. There is no better reason for living authentically than to live a life with the heart of our Savior. To live a life with the heart of Jesus also sounds very refreshing. And my encouragement to you here is to spend as much time as you can in your personal relationship with Jesus so that you can know His heart.

The WWJD bracelets reminded people to think, "What would Jesus do?" I think that I would like mine to read WWJHB, "What would Jesus' heart be?" This would help me to make all of my decisions with the thought, "What outcome will this bring?" Is this where the heart of Jesus would be? I think then I would be showing "unquestionable evidence" that I was living true to my origin. I would be authentic.

Finally, let me encourage you that if you are not already doing it, go and share your victories, joys, and struggles with a friend. It is very good for the soul, and will improve the authenticity of your life. My prayer is that anyone reading this will be able to fill their desire to be known and will know that this was written with the hope that the Spirit touches your heart in a personal way.

When I wrote this I also asked people, if they would, to respond to me how they were doing. I was pleased to see how many took me up on the offer. It was a combination of authenticity hitting a chord with them and being given the open door to share. It was one of those times when someone would say that they had just heard the same topic in church that week and how they went out to put it into practice. I felt that the Holy Spirit obviously was looking to get that message out to many.

OUR GREATEST NEED

04/10/2008

We often fail to grasp our greatest need in times of greatest need. When we are distressed, bewildered, threatened, shaken; in those moments when we want more than anything, God to do something; when we wonder, more than ever, if there even is a God to do anything—in those moments of greatest need, our greatest need is simply to see the Lord. To see Him high and exalted. To see Him in His kingly majesty. To see Him in His perfect holiness. Nothing else can so quickly put our life into right perspective, scale it to true proportion.

—Mark Buchanan, *The Holy Wild*

In an interview in the *Leadership Journal* (Spring 1997), Eugene Peterson said his most important job as a pastor on Sundays is to get up in the pulpit and say, "Let us worship God." He continued, "I cannot fail to call the congregation to worship God, to listen to His word, to offer themselves to God. Worship becomes a place where we have our lives redefined for us."

Is there a better way for us to have our lives redefined than to see God as He really is?

Seek Me that you may live.   —Amos 5:4

That sounds simple, doesn't it? "Seek Me that you may live," so that when we are in a time of "greatest need," that we would just look to see Him. But I was reminded this week by my daughter Stephanie of the story in Luke 24 about the men on the road to Emmaus. These men, miserable and confused after seeing Jesus crucified a few days previously, walked along and talked with Jesus and yet did not see that it was Him. These men were still lamenting about Jesus' death, even though they had been told about the empty tomb and the angels saying that Jesus was alive. Their problem was that they were still looking for Jesus as the one who would lead Israel militarily or politically. That was their answer to their greatest need. They were not looking to see Him as He really was: the Savior of the entire world! That was truly their greatest need.

What a great story for us today who strive to live a life of walking with God. What do we do when we find ourselves in times of great need? Most of us try and figure out how to solve the problem or need. Then, when that fails, we start praying for God to hurry up and fix our situation. Our first action should be to say, "Lord, please let me see you clearly. Please let me know that you are here with me so that I may worship You. For then, and only then, will I be fully equipped and ready to handle this need."

But seek first His kingdom and His righteousness...

—Matthew 6:33

So let me just encourage you now to see God. This is a simple reminder that when you are in that time of greatest need, your greatest need will be the need to focus your spiritual eyes to simply see the Lord. See Him as He really is.

Seek Him that you may live! See Him high and exalted. Worship Him. Then you will be ready to go through whatever lies ahead.

This may have been one of the shortest Wind-Fire Moments that I have written. But I find it that it was a message of simplicity, and that will often get right to the point. And it was a good reminder to people to remember to turn to God when times get tough.

TIME ALONE WITH GOD

10/23/2008

What if you had two or three hours alone with God? I mean really alone. No normal comforts or distractions. Just you and God. To me that sounds almost scary. Could I handle that long a time in worldly quiet, but Godly conversation?

Here is a picture: for the second time in a few weeks, I have found myself on an extensive road trip—some 1,200 miles in a 35-hour window, with more than half of that being spent in a 24-foot diesel box-truck with only a radio, on stretches of Oregon and Washington highways with little radio reception. It's a big truck, with a speed limiter at 65 mph. There are seemingly endless miles of black highway with few lights on the horizon. This is what I mean by alone and with few distractions: not in a hurry to get anywhere, not worried about my next turn or about weaving in and out of traffic. Just me, with the remnants of my McDonald's super-sized coke and some Sour Skittles to keep me company.

I should have been excited to have all that time alone with God, but actually I felt like I could not adequately fill that time. I'm kind of embarrassed to say it, but I was hesitant to think that I could fill that much time with direct conversation with my God. But after I realized all that that I needed to say and all that I need to hear, I could not have been proven more wrong.

I want to encourage you by challenging you to carve out a big chunk of time for God, and just see what happens with it. I mean find some *real*, unobstructed time, and I, for one, know that is hard to do. That is why I call this a challenge. I know that we all will spend time with God, like I spend a lot of time talking with Him while in the car. But I can get distracted by thinking about how soon I need to be somewhere. And while my constant listening to CDs while I drive can be a worship time with God, it also can be something that interferes with my conversation with Him. Probably the worst distraction of all is my getting mad at the driver who just moved right in front of me. Boldly proclaiming, "You moron!" kind of messes up my connection with the Spirit.

Let me remind you of a couple of cool things that come from having such a big block of time to give to Him:

Prayer for others: Start by praying through an extensive list of all the people you care about. When you are not in a hurry to get through this, you really take the time to pray in earnest. When you pause during the prayer for one person, you will find how the Holy Spirit communicates to you other things that you can be praying for.

This also gives you the chance to think of all the people that you have told, "Hey, I'll be praying for you," and never followed through on. Believe me, there are a lot of people you can be praying for, and they would really appreciate it.

Time for healing: Jesus said that He came to heal the brokenhearted, and there is no better way to find peace and relief from your struggles than to be quiet and let the Spirit completely drench you with His peace, comfort, and love.

Time for listening: This is one I have spoken about before, but a good portion of your prayer time should be in listening to the Spirit. This is a time for your heart to be charged up. It may sound intimidating to just get to that place where it can be very quiet. Like during the prayer time of a group study. Sometimes it is uncomfortable to sit there, waiting for the other person to talk. And when that other person is God, it is not your normal conversation.

But it should be normal conversation, shouldn't it? My point is, how can we not be excited to have a bunch of time to spend uninterrupted with God? Think about that. Why are so many of us hesitant to do this? I can think of a couple of reasons:

We are afraid that we will not hear from Him.

But Jesus says in John 10:27, *"My sheep hear My voice, and I know them, and they follow Me."* This is a promise that you will hear His voice. And of course, the reason that we begin to recognize a voice is because we have spent a lot of time talking to that person.

We are afraid that maybe what we hear will not be the voice of God.

Again, the way to overcome this is to personally know the voice of God, to spend so much time with Him that there is no question that it is His voice that is guiding you. Then you will not confuse it with your own thoughts or the whispers of the enemy. A friend of mine said just this week, "When my wife calls me on the phone, she doesn't have to identify herself and say, 'Hi, this is your wife.' She can just say 'hi' and start talking, because I know her voice."

I want to encourage you to grow to be comfortable in knowing His voice, and I want to challenge you to carve out that very large (and uncomfortable) amount of time with Him. Maybe some of you will be on a long airplane ride soon. That is a great place to get that unobstructed time. Why do think you hear of so many songs being written by someone who was staring out the window of a plane?

Let me end by giving you a little test to see how you would fare with recognizing His voice over your own or the whispers of the evil one. One statement is what you would hear from God, and the other might be your own or from the enemy:

"Nobody can spend that much time alone without doing something. You, especially, wouldn't have enough to say to God, and He really doesn't speak to *you*, anyway. And if you ever really could find that much time, you wouldn't spend it like that..."

"I'll wait for you. I would really love to hear your heart open up and to talk to Me for a while. I have so much that I want to share with you..."

This is one test you should not fail.

This Moment received a number of comments. One came from my (at the time) 16-year-old daughter, who said, "...maybe another reason [we hesitate to spend time with God] is if we really take time to listen to God, that means we have to surrender ourselves and our normal routine of thinking or 'pity party' and we're not in control. Maybe we're afraid of that."

CONFLICT

03/17/2011

I just spent a couple of days sitting through some leadership seminars that my company provided for us. The instructor for the two days was a high-energy gal who was a little over the top when it came to the arm waving and voice inflections, though I guess it did keep me awake. Instead of rebelling against her performance, though, I decided that I should have empathy for her role there, since I have had to try and keep the attention of groups before, and that I should be able to learn something from her.

I really did not expect to find inspiration from anything there that I would end up writing about, but it really should not surprise me that I did.

The instructor was talking about conflict and how each of us handles it. She mentioned that the old theory is that there are two ways to handle conflict: fight or flight. She asked us all which one we had more preference for, and my response was flight. I am not a big fan of conflict; it is one area in management and life that I need to be much better at. But the strange thing that she ended up sharing with us was that, regardless of whether we were in favor of fight or flight, both are really wrong.

Her point was that conflict does not have to be a bad thing—especially in the realm of managing people. Conflict can often be a sign that someone is passionate about a position and cares greatly for the situation. The converse would be apathy or fear that overtakes people so that they do not want to step up and stand their ground in support of their point or situation. The right choice here is to engage in finding a solution to the conflict by learning what is at the heart of the issue and in the hearts of the others involved.

My thoughts went immediately to our relationship with God and the fact that we can all run into our times of conflict with Him. Maybe we could use "challenge" in the place of the word conflict. Either way, it comes when we disagree with how we feel God is leading us, when He doesn't respond to prayer they way we would like, or we just grow discontent with our general lot in life.

And that brings us to the three J's of conflict in the Bible: Jacob, Jonah, and Job. One chose to fight (wrestle), one chose flight, and the other stood his ground and kept his emotions in check.

Jacob: In his decision to wrestle with God, he showed some passion, but he was also left with a lifelong disability as a reminder of his wrestling with God.

Jonah: I have been told that Nineveh was definitely not the place that any prophet or teacher of God would have had as his first choice for a weekend seminar on "Turning Your Lives Around," but Jonah should have known that there was nowhere that he could run that God would not find him. And so he found himself in the belly of the whale.

Job: My man Job decided to stand his ground in his troubling situation, to work it out with God. And while there was still a lesson for Job to learn in this, he did not succumb to cursing God and turning his back on Him, nor to arrogantly telling God that He had it all wrong.

How do you deal with God in situations of conflict? Do you ever choose to fight, or do you just find that it is easier to turn and avoid Him?

Deciding to fight makes almost every situation an emotional one. The speaker stated that when the emotion level goes up inside of you, there is a signal sent to the brain that starts shutting down the intelligence area. So if you are ever wondering why you make a questionable decision when you lose it emotionally, know that it is because you neurologically shut down your full access to your intelligence. When that happens, you don't have a chance.

And you don't have to look any further than Jonah to know that it is futile to try and run from God. Issues and problems will not go away by trying to ignore them, no matter how hard we hope they will.

This is why we must meet with God and go directly to the issue. We must seek His wisdom so that we will find answers, and if that is slow to come, then we must also seek the strength and peace to hold on. And by keeping our emotions in line as we learn to deal with a situation, we allow our minds to function properly, and we may be able to make wiser choices, not to mention that it will allow our hearts to be open to hear God's direction.

A friend shared with me that studies have recently shown that, while people's lives used to show patterns of periods of calm—still waters, you could say—and periods when they faced rough times, now society and the economy are creating a constant ride through whitewater rapids. Welcome to a world of constant conflict and challenge.

Like rafting down a river, our success will depend on how we position ourselves during the rough waters. We cannot just sit back, ignorant of what is going on around us. Sometimes you cannot fight against the current, and you must actually paddle with it. And again, fight or flight does not help the situation. We must engage with the conflict and see it through.

In the end though, the wonderful thing about God is always the same: He will love us through it all. Jacob, Jonah, and Job all continued on under His great love and with blessings. So whether it is fight, flight, or a little more manageable tactic, our God is there in the midst of our conflicts and challenges with Him, and afterwards, to carry us forward.

This writing came out after I had told people that there would be a book. One of the responses to this one was that it definitely should go into the book. So I took the advice and made a late switch to put it in here. A pastor friend said it reminded him of the proverb [Prov. 10:19] that says that where there are a lot of words, sin is inevitable. He said that we must be careful of those high-octane, emotional moments where we need to be watchful of the things we say.

WHAT INSTEAD OF WHY

07/02/2009

As I started to write in my journal, I began, "Wednesday, July 1, 2009. A new month. A new day. What am I to do with it, Lord?"

Back in May a few of us got the opportunity to share some hospitality by providing lunch for the musicians Brandon Heath, Third Day, and Revive. Mac Powell and Brandon asked if they could hear my story of becoming a partner in the winery we were hosting them at. They had a wonderful sincerity about them that inspired me to spend the last couple of months asking other people if I could hear their stories. I have been blessed to have gotten the time to visit with a number of people, most of whom I did not really know. It has been awesome! But I found myself wondering, "Lord, what do I do with all these stories?"

Then the Spirit nudged me with the thought that we, as believers, often spend a lot of sedentary faith time asking *why* questions to God. We are an age of "Why? Believers." And so I am here to encourage us all this week to focus on becoming more proactive in our faith, becoming an age of "What? Believers." We should be asking God, "What is it, Lord, that you want us to do with this?"

You see, we can waste a lot of time *and heart* asking *why*. The *why* might be as simple as, *It just happened that way.* Was the bicycle accident I recently heard about something that God had orchestrated, or was it just a random accident, with no rhyme or reason to it? Either way, the bottom line from God is: "What are you going to do with it?"

And even if a situation is from "Divine Intervention" to some extent, the bottom line from God is still the same: "Now that you have seen Me move, what is your response going to be?"

God will move and do mighty things for us, but He created us to be a part of this adventure. We have an active role, and it is not to be critic, judge, or kibitzer from the sidelines. I have a feeling that the person who coined the phrase, *When life [God] gives you lemons, make lemonade,* first sat around for a while asking *why,* until he figured out that the answer was really in the *what am I going to do with my situation?*

Think of all the *whys* that we ask:

Why is this relationship that way?

Why are we struggling so much financially?

Why did this person have to pass away?

Why did I make that decision that went awry?

Why did I start losing my hair at such a young age? (Oops, I don't know how that one got in here.)

There are so many of those questions we can hang onto out there, and since we may never be given the answer (down here), the bottom line needs to be, *What are you going to do with that situation?* Whether the circumstance is divinely given or just something that happens in this life of free will, God wants to know how you are going to respond.

He wants to know if you are going to have an active faith and step up to it. Just think of the people's lives around you that you could have a positive impact on if you starting acting in the *what would you have me do* mode—not to mention the impact on your own life.

I will often ask God, "What is going on here?" I do so in hope that He will reveal something to me about a troubling situation. The enemy often works his deception to create turmoil and situations that we just can't figure out, and we need God to reveal that which is not of Him. But once we receive some revelation, it should always be followed with a proactive, "Lord, what will you have me do now?"

So let me encourage you by giving you permission to ask *what.* It is then that you will most likely see God move in a great and mighty way!

One person responded to this by saying that she was inspired to begin to check herself to see how often she was asking why, *instead of boldly asking herself and God,* what. *She was going to go off for a hike that weekend and was now anxious to see what God might have to say.*

THE UNEXPECTED

05/28/2009

When I joined my small men's group that meets every other Tuesday night, I discovered that they had a little ritual: after a short chatting time, there was a call for an opening prayer. But instead of saying, "Who wants to open us in prayer tonight," everyone started raising a thumb. Yes, you get it. The last one to put up a thumb was the one who had to pray. Not trying to be a party-pooper, I said that I didn't really like that game. I didn't think it should come down to *who* **has** *to pray*; it should be *who* **gets** *to pray*. So most evenings I do my quiet boycott of the game, and the other guys end up sitting there with their silly grins, looking at me, each one with a thumb in the air. (Men are just grown-up boys, and it is always about games and competition!) But, hey, I *get* to pray...

This last time together, the Spirit in the midst of my prayer gave me something new to add: *"and may your Spirit deliver to us tonight something that none of us can even expect."*

We are always asking God for something, but what we ask for is always limited to what we can think of at the time. So why not go off the board and ask for something special that you cannot plan for, much less imagine?

And the Spirit delivered big time! It was one of the best discussion nights that the group had experienced in many months. One of the men led us through a wonderful message he had recently read, and with that came deep sharing and numerous times when men would speak out affirmation to each other in order to contradict the self-view that someone was sharing. There were a few times when someone would say, "Why are you saying that you are weak in this area? I see you as one of the most gifted people in this area, and you have impacted many people with your strength and the way you reflect God's glory."

Then the Spirit would move the person to discuss aloud why he might have had those thoughts of weakness in that area of his life. New strength and perspectives were found throughout the night. It was a night in which God answered us in a way that was *unexpected*. It was powerful! It was the way that these nights should be, and maybe we had grown too comfortable with our times together to expect such an evening.

So let me encourage you to add the petition of the unexpected to your conversations with God. Who knows what and where God will choose to deliver to you?

I know some of you might be thinking, "Jim, I think you've finally lost it this time." But when you look at the simplicity of asking for the unexpected, it all makes sense, doesn't it? And I must tell you that there is something uniquely special to making such a request. It is not just another spin on how to do your everyday prayer. What the Spirit has shown me here, is a different joy and appreciation of the love I have for the Father, where I am not just thanking Him for answering something specific that I have asked for (the things which we hope for and expect), but I am instead being grateful and amazed with something that came without hope or expectation.

It should not come as a complete surprise that God can deliver this to you. Job 37:5 says,

God thunders with His voice wondrously, doing great things which we cannot comprehend.

And Philippians 4:7 talks to us about the "peace of God, which surpasses all comprehension."

If there is so much about our marvelous God that we cannot comprehend to begin with, then there is much out there for us that we are just unable to anticipate. God's ways are greater than our ways—and thank You, God, for that.

Go ahead and try it. Put in your petition. Then all that you have to do is to be ready and able to recognize it. Great or small things, just watch...

He will show up!

This Moment elicited a number of responses. One appreciated it as a reminder to seek the Lord's agenda. Another person said it came at a very opportune moment. This person was leading a group of people through a time of career transition and thought

that to "petition the unexpected" should be part of that group's motto. It also brought out the notion of having trust in the Lord, that He can bring us that which is beyond our expectations.

—SECTION THREE—

EYES OF THE HEART

These six reflections deal with using your heart to see and feel the moments in life that God has to offer us.

I hope that these writings show a true reflection of God in the recognition of that which is around us. They have a certain intimacy to them that could only come from opening the eyes of the heart to the inspiration of the Spirit. I noticed in reading them again myself, that I often went into the writing not knowing how I might get a message across or even what I would say.

But, as He always does, God came through with a message to share. My hope, as always, is that you will be encouraged.

HIGH PLACES
07/10/2008

Though the fig tree should not blossom, and there be no fruit on the vines; though the yield of the olive should fail, and the fields produce no food; though the flock should be cut off from the fold, and there be no cattle in the stalls... Yet I will exult in the Lord, I will rejoice in the God of my salvation... The Lord God is my strength, and He has made my feet like hinds' feet, and He makes me walk on high places.

—Habakkuk 3:17–19

I have always loved this scripture about having "hinds' feet" and being set on "high places." I think it all started after reading Hannah Hurnard's book, *Hinds' Feet on High Places,* when I was really young. I guess it just sounded cool to go to high places and be able to spring like a deer to get up the mountain. But I never really grasped the application to my spiritual life until looking into it this week.

These "high places" are where we go to worship to God in the most personal and intense way. God not only calls us to an elevated place of worship, but He gives us the ability (the hinds' feet) to get there. There is something special for us there if we make the journey, something that we desperately need.

And get this: we are to go there not only when our lives are filled with blessings but also when all seems to have been lost or when our vision of the path for our life is so cloudy that we cannot find our way. In both situations, we are to worship Him and to know that He is good. Yes, these high places are very unique places in deed.

The Spirit has revealed to me this week a couple of reasons that He calls me to my high places:

God wants me in a higher place because I can see differently from there. Is this not why we hike miles up a mountainside, fly in small planes, or go up in a hot-air balloon? We want to see more. We want to see as God sees. In these high places, I not only see more as God sees, but I am also better able to see God Himself. And then I worship Him.

From these high places, I should be more aware, better able to see the vision of God's larger story and how it dwarfs the little stories that I allow myself to get caught up in. I need to see things differently.

I need to be able to stop and recognize the dealings of the enemy against my spiritual heart, so that I will not be taken out in my quest to fulfill the role that God has for me in His story. And I need to be able to climb high and appreciate things that I have come to take for granted, for from that height, I can see them in a new light. All the while, I aim to see God clearer and to worship Him.

Make me aware, make me see
Everything that I am is not about me
Take my world, turn it around
So that the obvious can be finally found
  —"Aware" by Salvador

But I also understand that my "high places" are a place I must go to learn to accept those things that I cannot, with my human thought process, otherwise accept. We all have been, at some time in our lives, in a place where we wonder about the fairness of life, or where we wonder where God is and why He seemingly won't answer our prayers in our time of need.

This week the question of fairness came up at our house. A very good friend of my youngest daughter lost her father (44 years old) to a sudden heart attack. In an instant, without warning, two children lose their dad, a wife loses her husband, parents lose a child. I will not even begin to pretend to understand the pain and devastation of this type of loss. But I know that in a similar situation, God would call on me to use my hinds' feet to reach my high places and worship Him.

When my life is hanging by a thread, and I think about the things you said
That in this moment seems so far away
Help me see the guarantees that first brought me to believe

So that I can make it through another day
Make me aware... make me see

My life has unfortunately endured that which was described in Habakkuk. I have gone through periods where the fig tree did not blossom, the fields did not produce, and there were no cattle in the stalls. In these days I encountered times when I lost sight of how I would make it through a situation, where I could barely see to take my next step, much less know where I was going to end up.

But it was in this time that I discovered the power of my hinds' feet, and I was able to make it to a place where I found a new level to my personal faith in God. It was a place where I had to give up all control of my situation and trust that God would take care of me. The richness of my relationship with Him that developed from this was new and extreme. I found that I was able to worship Him with a greater understanding of who He is, for I knew that He is good.

I then could understand and live out what Mark Buchanan, author of *The Holy Wild*, called one of the "best and deepest lessons that I have learned as a pastor, as a Christian, as a man: *The need to know God so well, that even though He slay me, yet I will worship Him. For He is good...*"

I now understand that I was able to reach this new level in my faith because "the Lord is my strength, and my God made my feet like hinds' feet and He *made* me walk in my high places." I also believe that until someone is taken to their high place of total surrender, he or she cannot experience the richness of the relationship to God that is found there.

My encouragement to you is that you find your own "high places" to go to, and I challenge you to go there. I pray that you may find a new richness of faith and worship there. And I have no doubt it will be so personal that others will not be able to fully appreciate what you have learned and what you have seen. These high places are for our personal relationships with our Heavenly Father.

For He is good, and the view is amazing...

This has always been one of my very favorite writings because I love the concept of the High Places. It has carried me through tough times and inspired me to live in a more intimate place with God. And when I had asked some people I knew, what were some of their favorite Moments that they thought should go into this book, this one was mentioned by many.

BLACK & WHITE VISION

12/02/2010

I was reading the sports page on Thanksgiving morning and came across a little article that talked about an ex-major-league baseball player who had passed away. His name was Danny McDevitt. No, I had never heard of him either. He pitched the last game for the Brooklyn Dodgers that was played at old Ebbets Field in Brooklyn in 1957, just before the team moved to Los Angeles.

Normally, I wouldn't have paid any attention to a story about an athlete I'd never heard of, but this one caught my eye because I wish I would have been able to see a game in that old, oddly shaped ballpark that hosted some of best-known baseball legends of yesteryear. I have seen a few film clips of games that were played back then and read articles about the stadium. So I sat and tried to imagine what that last game there was like.

I imagined a black-and-white picture of people playing in old, baggy uniforms. I saw some older men move in herky-jerky motions (isn't everyone in old film clips always kind of old-looking?) The crowd was dressed in all their dim and drab clothing. I was imagining this game in the only way I have memory of that time: in black-and-white.

But what was reality? It would have been in living color! The grass of the field was green that day, not grey. Danny McDevitt was only a 25-year-old athlete—a little older than my kids—not an older guy who needed Geritol to make it through his day. The uniforms were still baggy, but there was the bright blue of the Dodgers' baseball caps. The billboards on the outfield wall were in full color. It would look like just going to any other game today at some older minor league ballpark. The peanut vendors two sections over, shouting above the low murmur of the crowd, and the bags probably only cost a dime or a nickel. You could probably hear some creaks in the foundation of the stadium.

Now that I have truly got a picture of what it was really like, the game has become almost vivid to me. I really wish that I could have been there.

I want to encourage us to think about those areas (or events) in our lives that we picture in a particular way simply because we have based our vision only on what we think we know. What events in history are you limiting because of how you have chosen to picture them?

And back in the present, what have you been afraid to try and who have you been unsure of meeting, simply because you have only a biased vision of what it is or who they are? How many of you are living with a black-and-white view of things, when we really live in a full-color world?

What are you limiting in the stories told from the Bible?

I might as well be current with the Christmas season this week and start with this: Do you realize how old Mary was when she had this baby? She was so young. And with very mature steps, she and Joseph handled what was a scandalous situation in those times. And how small was that stable, really? Was it cold? What did it smell like? Take off your history blinders, and see this event in living color!

And what do you think the shepherds really saw in the night as the angel appeared and "the glory of the Lord shone around them" (Luke 2:9)? I know that they were told not to be afraid, so it wasn't just a casual drop-by. And how about when suddenly there appeared a multitude of the heavenly host, praising God? Can't you just jump into the moment here and be psyched over that? For all of you skeptics, you would have loved to be there, because what more proof do you want to see than that?

My point is, don't miss out on the real Christmas story this year. As you hear song after song, use that right side of your brain to make each story being sung about come alive to you. Turn up the color on the playback channel in your mind, see the people for who they really were, and take a moment to think about what they were truly feeling in that moment, when all they had to go on was the words of the prophets.

This can be a way to think about any past event, whether historical or something in your own lifespan. What are you missing out on by not embracing memory in full color?

Who have you chosen not to meet?

I think it is important to apply this idea to our daily lives. It may not be just our thoughts and memories of long ago that are limited to black-and-white, but we may have chosen to live in a world here and now that is void of color.

Are there people out there whom you have chosen not to get to know, just because of limited "clips" that you have heard about them? Sometimes we just don't have enough information to truly know how someone will be, or maybe we remember something that a person did years ago and we have set that picture in stone. It might be time to forgive someone or to go and see if that person has changed... maybe even as much as you have.

What have you limited yourself to experience?

Finally, are we living our faith in full, vivid color? Or have we chosen to not take certain steps in our lives because it is just easier to live a life devoid of passion? I think we could all be surprised at how merely living out "steps of faith" can bring passion and color to our relationship with God. All of us film-watchers remember the "step of faith" in *Indiana Jones and the Last Crusade*. Sometimes it is just the first step that is the hardest to take.

I know this might be a little out-of-the-box thinking, but I believe that the concept is very simple. Whether it is what you are remembering from the past or how you are ready to deal with today, see it for how it is (was), and live a life full of "color"!

The responses to this WFM were all over the place, possibly because I covered a lot of area. One person wrote about being encouraged to work on shyness and to step out to know more about people. One was challenged to imagine Mary as a teenager. A baseball fan enjoyed picturing Ebbets field. And my youngest daughter said, "I liked that one," which to me meant that I had done well.

And one other person, who picked up on thinking about how we see and judge others, made the point that no one lives with the facts: we all live with the story we tell ourselves about the facts.

THE COVERING

01/15/2009

In the first few weeks of December in 2008, Seattle experienced a series of snow storms that made me think we were stuck in the middle of *The Lion, the Witch, and the Wardrobe*, and the White Witch had made it forever winter. I know we in the Puget Sound area don't know what a real winter is, like the people in parts of the Midwest do, but that snow just kept coming and coming, covering all that I was used to seeing. I got the sense that, because I could no longer see certain colors, shapes, or direction, that something was missing.

Our winery has about eight acres. There's a lovely hillside with a gravel road that goes up the middle of the property to the Estate House. I love walking that path, but I also just like to look at it sometimes. I think it gives me comfort. And suddenly, it was gone under the snow. Not only couldn't I see it anymore, buried under the blanket of white, but walking up to the house became a difficult effort.

What I want to talk about here is a heart checkup. What things would your heart really miss if they were covered up or removed? Let me encourage you to take an inventory of the things your heart looks forward to seeing all the time, and find a way to remind yourself to take time to appreciate them.

Another thing that this snow covering did was to make me wonder about things I had never taken the time to look at before. I drove one of my daughter Stephanie's friends home from town because I had the Four-wheel-drive that day. This friend lives within a mile or two of us, but this day I took a different street to get to his home: a street no more than one block away from where I would normally turn. I was intrigued by driving through this unfamiliar neighborhood, trying to imagine what it looked liked on a normal day. I told Stephanie about my musings, and she said, "Mom said the exact same thing when we picked him up." We have lived in the same house for almost 20 years and had never been to this area so close to us, had never found out what there is around us.

What things in your life are like this? What would you find right there next to you if you took a little extra time to stray outside your normal routine? Is there a person you have never taken the time to get to know? Or, worse, someone you do know whom you have never made the effort to learn more about, to learn what makes them come alive. So I encourage you to take a turn down a different street. It's fun to go exploring, especially if you find something unique and special about someone else.

Finally, not only did this snow do a complete job of covering everything up, but it also brought some problems with it and left some destruction behind. But I was reminded that out of distress we can find little blessings:

The parking lot at the winery got so bad that our Four-wheel-drive was getting stuck, and of course, that meant no customers coming in the door. Then on the Saturday after the snow stopped, we asked a neighboring business if we could get the name of the people who had the Bobcat that just plowed their lot that morning. It turned out to be theirs, and right away they said they would come down to plow our lot for us. They were happy to help us and didn't ask for anything in return. As soon as they were done with the plowing, customers started pulling in.

All the snow that made it hard to get out of our neighborhood meant that it kept the college-age kids who were home for Christmas huddled together at the house more. If someone did venture out in the Four-wheel-drive, it became a group mission. And then, on Christmas Day, we were without power from 4 a.m. to 6 p.m., due to a snow-laden tree falling on a power line. It made for a unique Christmas: we cooked oatmeal and soup on the woodstove and played games together. I feel blessed, having a family who thrived in that situation.

Last but not least, my wife's hardworked yard of unique plants and beautiful trees took a beating. Major limbs broke off trees, and several of the plants did not recover. But the next Sunday, we went out to chainsaw and pile up some of the debris. We even cleared some areas to bring in more sunlight that will enhance the growth of the plants below. It was a fun day to be outside together, to accomplish a lot with some hard work, and also to come away with the hope of the restoration that later came to our tortured little garden of Eden.

The promise of restoration—I love that! It is a great reminder to all of us about the wonderful gift from our Savior to us. And we can always use that sort of reminder.

This definitely inspired emotions from many people who live up here in the Seattle area and were going through some of those same situations. I hope that even if I live in a much warmer climate, I can appreciate the visual and be encouraged by the message of restoration.

HEADING TOWARDS THE LIGHT

10/01/2009

It was just after six in the morning. I was freshly showered, though I cannot say that I was fresh in energy or spirit. Armed with a Starbucks coffee in my cup-holder, I entered the on-ramp to Eastbound Interstate 84, leaving Hood River, Oregon, for what was to be my four-and-a-half-hour drive to Spokane, Washington. I accelerated onto the freeway as another car came roaring by in the outside lane. I think that he was going a little fast, but out of a sense of proper community, I felt it my place that I should try to keep up. It was dark, and it was rainy, just the way that it had been when I pulled into the town the night before, after surviving the currents of water that had built up in the grooves of the highway. There wasn't much reason that anyone could be looking forward to beginning this early-morning drive, but I was excited. I told you that I was eastbound, didn't I? I was heading towards the Light.

I have had a few opportunities this year to speak to breakfast gatherings of Christian businesspeople. The title of my presentation for these events is, "Walking with God through a Never-Ending Jungle." I am told that the uniqueness to my talk is that there is no nice little ending to the story. Most people who get up to give a motivational talk will tell of the trials they have endured and how God has now brought them nicely to the other side, but my story seems to be bound in the middle of some trilogy. I have to be honest that when this particular journey began, I felt that I could handle God's little mini-series for this chapter of my life—I just didn't realize that He had signed me up for a long-running series that seems to get renewed every year.

This journey through the dark and the rain felt symbolic of my journey over the last number of years. I continued to drive because I had somewhere to go, but it was the knowledge that I was heading toward the light and the promise of clearing skies that had me excited.

We all travel on our own unique journeys, and it is my hope to encourage you to stay strong in your journey, to celebrate all that is good and to endure the rough spots that come your way. Here are some things I noticed on my drive to Spokane that might be helpful to you:

There is Community all around us, living out stories.

Going through an overpass area near the next town, I was struck by the sight of all the red lights on the back of the semi-trucks that had been parked overnight at a rest stop: weary travelers, traveling the highways day after day. They were just finishing up their rest and going back to work, but they had spent the evening surrounded by others doing the same thing.

We need to recognize that we are not traveling alone. We may have different circumstances that take us in different directions, but we also need a time when we can come together. We will be the stronger for it.

Be careful of putting your life on cruise control.

Cruise control can be a very nice thing. I used it a lot on my journey. But early in the morning I encountered a few cars that seemed to be traveling down the fast lane a little oblivious to everyone else around them. They would occasionally drift to the center of the lane and then correct themselves. Sure, they were going forward, but they seemed a little dazed.

Cruise control has its purposes, but if we live our lives in cruise control mode, we may not be aware of how we are affecting others. We must be careful to avoid getting stuck doing things one way and at one speed, or we may lose our awareness and become unable to adapt if it becomes necessary to deviate from our course.

There will be detours.

I was in the middle of nowhere, with no clue of my surroundings, and I found my main path blocked. "Road Closed! Do not enter! Take alternate routes!" I had no idea of an alternate route, but luckily there were detour signs. So I was led on a very unfamiliar path. I had no guarantee that this was going to bring me back to where I needed to be, but I followed with the expectation that the ones in charge were not leading me astray.

That is how my life has seemed to go over the last eight years. Just when I settle comfortably on a path, God allows, or possibly even constructs, a little detour. Often I have no clue of where the next turn on the path is going to come, but I follow in faith that the One who has created me and who heals and takes care of my heart is not leading me astray.

Celebrate the good and handle the rest.

My drive to Spokane gave me beautiful views of the Columbia River and eastern Washington wheat fields, with some gorgeous moments of completely clear skies. I celebrated and praised my Father for all that I've been given. And throughout the day, I was given glimpses of clouds on the horizon, and I was ready. Again, this has been my journey.

Later in the day, about 7 p.m., I was heading west on Interstate 90, making my way past Ellensburg on my way home. That day was a journey of some 700 miles of highway driving sandwiched around a successful business day in Spokane. I had enjoyed the beauty of Eastern Washington and the warmth of the day. As I looked ahead to the west, the sky was dark with intensely black clouds. I was heading into what would be a torrential downpour over Snoqualmie Pass, but I knew that on the other side of those clouds, the sun was beginning to set.

I was excited! It was evening, and I was westbound. Dark clouds in my way or not, I would stay the course and head towards the Light.

Many people said that they were happy to have been taken on the ride with me, and I hope that you enjoyed it as well. Life is a journey, and even with its unplanned-for bumps, it is always worth stepping forward and keeping our eyes wide open to what God has in store.

To See is to Believe

02/10/2011

Someone once said to me, "You keep me well-rooted in God and challenge me on what I should *see* versus what I *feel*." Of course, I thought that was an awesome thing for someone to say, but I was actually a little confused by it. Being the hopeless romantic that that I am, I feel that I am all about emotion and feeling.

But I knew that what he was sharing was right from his heart, and that it was a very good thing. In a later exchange, he told me, "To *see* is to believe; feeling (sometimes) can be misconstrued." He went on to say that just recently he had felt good about helping a particular woman, but it was not until he looked and saw God in her eyes and heart that he fully realized what God had in store for them in that moment.

A short time later, I heard these lines from "Now More than Ever," by Brandon Heath, which drove home to me the power of seeing:

Dig my hands into the earth
Sometimes I need You so bad, it hurts
I want you now more than ever
The more I see, the more I want
The more I know, it doesn't stop
Your beauty speaks to call me home
Now more than ever

I want to encourage us all to see with the eyes of the heart. And in my encouragement, let me aspire to live up to the words of Philemon 4–7, which have been shared to me over the last couple of weeks from two different people:

I thank my God, always making memories of you in my prayers, because I hear of your love and of the faith which you have toward the Lord Jesus and toward all of the saints; and I pray that the fellowship of your faith may become effective through the knowledge of every good thing which is in you for Christ's sake. **For I have come to have much joy and comfort in your love, because the hearts of the saints have been refreshed through you, brother.**

If you do not look, you will not see. You have to love the simplicity of that statement. That is a real, wondrous thing about God. He is always there. He is in everything, and it is up to me to look, so that I may find Him in the beauty which is to be found in creation, like the light of a breaking day.

I often go into Seattle early (to beat traffic) and then take some time to get a coffee and get some of my writing in. I have this great place where I sit in the corner and can look west to the Olympic Mountains and east to the Cascades. I watch as the city goes from dark to light. The world changes before my eyes. Many people pass through this spot I have chosen to watch from, some just starting their days and others getting ready to finish.

God can also be seen in the stretched cheeks of excitement on the child who is running through the grocery store with joy and wonder, talking to her mom or dad about what is going on. I love watching those moments. Or how about the bright eyes that shine in the face of someone who is glad to see you? Doesn't that just do your soul some good?

In a very early Wind-Fire Moment, I wrote about finding "God moments." They are happening all the time around you, and your ability to see them comes down to if you are taking the time to look.

You can look and see the hearts of others. To appease my hopeless romantic spirit, I have to quote something from one of the corniest chick flick/ romantic comedies that nevertheless makes my heart feel good. In *Win a Date with Tad Hamilton*, Pete (my hero) is hopelessly in love with Rosalee, who is also his best friend. Pete knows that she has six different smiles: 1) when something flat-out makes her laugh, 2) when she laughs out of politeness, 3) when she makes plans, 4) when she makes fun of herself, 5) when she is uncomfortable, and 6) when she is talking about her friends. Wouldn't you want someone to see this much in you?

Of course, Rosalee rejects his love at first, because it wouldn't be your classic romantic comedy without that kind of conflict. Then, upon realizing that she does love him, she attempts (in one of my most favorite scenes) to get him back by telling him that he has five smiles: "Pete, do you know that you have five smiles? One, when you think someone's an idiot. One, when you think someone is a real idiot. One, when you get all dressed up. One, when you are signing Barry White. And one. . . when you are looking at me."

Maybe I annoy the guys at my breakfast table every Wednesday morning as my eyes are always on the move to see what is happening around the restaurant. But what I am doing is watching people as they come in. I often look to see if there is any joy in their spirit. I am watching the servers as they go about their work. Are they happy today, or do they look a little tired and worn? Is their hair a different color or style (sorry, I am a closet fashionista)? Depending on the situation, it might just take a comment or question to start an authentic conversation. People like to know that they are being seen and being seen in such a way that they know others care about how they are doing.

That is what I believe Paul was writing about in his salutations to Philemon. "Thank you for seeing others. Thank you for seeing what it is needed to refresh their hearts." And we are not able to really see others if we are not taking time to seek out God and what He is doing. Then we are able to see with His eyes, and our hearts become fully alive to a wonderful world opened up to us.

This one seemed to resonate with a lot of people. For some, they too enjoy watching other people. Others were inspired by the idea of having eyes to see, and they would now be taking time to look upon others in a more intent way. One of my friends from my breakfast group said it did not annoy him that I "read the room," but that it amuses and interests him.

ADVENTURE

03/25/2010

I climb into my car and slide behind the wheel. Door shut, seat belt fastened, key in the ignition: I am in place, just like an astronaut ready for take-off or Special Agent 007 ready to roll. I turn on the engine, and it's just me, alone in my car, heading off to some destination. Immediately, I have to make the choice between quiet thought and prayer or a little sound to inspire my heart or stimulate my brain. There are four things I am inclined to turn on when I am not in the solitude mode: sports radio banter, the Christian radio station, music on CD, and books or sermons on CD or cassette tape (yes, those do still exist), which are usually from John Eldredge. Recently, when I drove to Los Angeles, I threw a series of cassettes from an Eldredge retreat into my son's car to accompany me through 22 hours of driving, only to realize, once on the road, that the car I was in didn't have a tape player. Oh well, I would have only three sound options for the trip, except for when talking-to-myself mode reached audible levels.

John Eldredge often speaks of the "adventure to live" as a main theme in the story/heart of every man or woman. (Actually, he will usually use "an adventure to share" in the context of the story/heart of a woman, but since I live with some independent and strong-willed ladies, I do not put a distinction between the two.) Recently, I went through an interview process for the director position at a Christian camp, and the word adventure came up there, too, in the context of camp experience for both campers and staff.

My desire is to inspire us all to find adventure in places that we might not normally see it, to take the areas in our life that may seem problematic, scary, uncharted, or maybe just plain boring, and to think of a way to turn it into an adventure. There is something deep in our hearts that wants to take the risk or to be heroic. So take a look at life this week and see if there is an adventure waiting for you:

To do what you are afraid of. For people who have the fear of going out and being around others, this could be a trip to Starbucks to get some coffee. Something that is common to some could be an adventure into fear for others. I always think of my friend Jim when the topic of overcoming fear comes up. He conquered his fear of heights by taking an adventure and going skydiving. That might sound a little radical to you, but when we allow fears in our life to hold us back from truly living, then we must think of gearing up for an adventure that will not only stir our hearts but may change our lives forever.

As a side note, there may be something that you are not "afraid" of doing but that you fear not doing well enough (or being wrong), and that keeps you from trying. What starts with being the kid in school who hesitates to raise a hand, carries on into adulthood when we are hesitant to contribute in a Bible study. We fear not only that may we say something wrong but that we may reveal more of ourselves than we are prepared to do. Just remember, you cannot be wrong when you are only sharing your perception or how you feel.

To go where you have not yet gone. If you have ever wanted to join the crew of the Starship *Enterprise*, "to boldly go where no man has gone before," this is for you. I have always admired those who pick up a backpack and head off to a foreign country, or even just to other parts of America. That is one exciting way to explore new places. For others, it may be to try a new career or to enter into a new chapter of life: moving away from home, getting married, raising children, or heading into retirement. Taking this step into the unknown is responding to something inside of us that says that there is more out there. And just maybe we were created to be part of something bigger than what we have allowed ourselves so far.

To find what you are searching for. Think of Indiana Jones searching for the Ark of the Covenant or the Holy Grail. He was completely focused on what he was after. Maybe your adventure will be like that, or maybe it will be more like Ray Kinsella in *Field of Dreams*, who at the end, came to realize that his quest was to recapture a lost opportunity to play catch with his dad.

It may be an adventure that takes on epic spiritual proportions, where you begin a journey to know God for who He really is and meet Him right in the midst of where you are living. But beware of ending up like Bono and U2, who apparently "still haven't found what they're looking for." I would caution anyone from getting lost in an adventure that has no real direction and purpose just for the sake of adventure. For it is when there is great purpose, as for Frodo and the rest of the Fellowship of the Ring, that great strength can be found and great obstacles overcome. This also brings up the importance of having community to be there for you, even if it is in the background.

I find a wonderful theme to all of these. Adventure is to allow us all to become greater in our true and intended glory, to fulfill and live out a life that has been designed in us by our creator. There is something inside that calls us to live out adventure—and it is never too late. No matter what age you might be or what place in life you are in, there is something that can be an adventure for you. It might be as simple as starting to write something or reaching out to that person who may need a friend. All that may be asked of you is just a small leap in faith.

I know that it inspires me, and I hope that it inspires you!

Many people were inspired by the thoughts of adventure and found them to be very powerful. To what adventure are you called? It is out there, and you don't have to get into your car and drive for a thousand miles to find it. It is about being aware and being ready. God will deliver.

—SECTION FOUR—

THE JOURNEY

When I have had the privilege to speak in front of Christian business leaders, my topic has been "Walking with God through a Never-Ending Jungle." I tell a story that has no ending, which, as a good friend told me, is somewhat messy. And from what I have been told, the messages have been very well received because they are delivered with an authentic heart to people who are going through struggles and career changes.

The following eight pieces are at the heart of the trip through the Jungle and have prompted a lot of feedback. I hope that you will hear authenticity in these words, and maybe you will find yourselves saying, "I am not the only one who feels that way; I'm not the only one who has spent time struggling."

And I hope that you will be encouraged, because the message is always the same: God is good and He carries us through, whether we have a good idea of where we are going or can barely figure out where our next step should be. He will carry us through.

Two Parts Easy, One Part Hard

07/15/2010

We've all heard this riddle before: "What weighs more, a hundred pounds of bricks or a hundred pounds of feathers?"

"Oh, I get it. They weigh the same."

Well, here's a new equation. Which weighs more, two parts easy or one part hard? Let me put it another way, since the word *easy* might be misconstrued. How about, two parts good or one part bad?

As someone who lives with a high-school science teacher, I know what you scientific thinkers are saying right now. "You haven't given us all the data yet. What is the measurement of the easy, and how hard is the hard?" I say to you, it doesn't really matter.

I encountered this new equation early one morning as I was driving off to a breakfast of Christian businesspeople. I kept the music and talk radio off and just talked with God:

"God, thank you for a beautiful morning, and I pray for something great today. I am tired of going so long without a regular job, and I am really ready for this chapter of my life to end. I pray that I will meet someone today who will be a link to a job opportunity. I pray for something unexpectedly wonderful. God, I can't imagine how I would get through this without You here with me. But in the same instant, it is hard. And it kind of seems strange that I do have to continue to go through it, knowing that You are here for me. What do I do with that, God?"

I paused a little to actually listen.

"OK, I guess I can handle two parts easy and one part hard."

I think that may be my new life motto.

I struggle a bit when I am asked, "How are you doing?" I stop for a moment because I want to refrain from a token answer of, "Fine." I mean, some of life is really good: every week I get to write a message that the Holy Spirit has given me inspiration for, so that I can attempt to encourage the hearts of others. I have a great community around me, and my family is loving and supportive. I love being alive.

On the other hand, the way things are in regards to being without work and struggling financially is really crappy. I am tired of the constant stress and strain, and I don't know what unknown thing will finally make things better.

Life right now is two parts easy and one part hard.

Which gets me back to my original question. Which one weighs more? I guess the best answer to this is, *It depends on the day*. Sometimes it just depends on the moment.

I'm sure many of you can relate to that.

My encouragement to you this week is to remember that life is both easy and hard. It is filled with both good and bad. If I was going to have to say which weighs more, I would have to go with the hard. So what are we to do about that?

Give your burdens over to Him: Sometimes the weight of carrying our problems can make us feel like we are going through the day as Quasimodo, or that we are the camel, just waiting for that last straw that will break our back. This weight can be from a long-time wound, a broken relationship, sin-laden guilt, or maybe just rough financial times. Whatever the source, it can feel far too heavy to carry alone. If we do not fully surrender everything over to Him, we will crumble and the recovery process will take even longer.

Take it from me, though, totally surrendering your life (and I mean *totally*) does not make the problems immediately go away. But it will extremely lighten the load so that you can walk upright again. And it will help to bring you into intimate community with the Trinity, and that is what will lead you fully into the two parts easy.

This is an equation that can only be explained by faith. The scales will always be tipped in favor of the side that holds the two parts easy. That is just the way that God works. It is really hard to try to explain to people, because the reality of the hard is what is so visible.

The very next day, I was off to Tacoma to speak in front of another group of

Christian businesspeople. I told them of my walk with God through a never-ending jungle, the somewhat messy story that has no end to it yet. There is only hope. But I ended that talk the way I always end my talks on that subject, with the same lasting message: "God is good. Life is good."

I'll take the two parts easy, please...

If "The Lemonade Stand" is my signature Moment for just seeing God in the simple everyday life stories, this one has stood out as the signature to the "life is hard" category. Maybe it is just the title that people relate to, but this writing solicited a number of responses.

CALLED TO DO

01/20/2011

I was listening to the message of a good friend at a breakfast gathering of Christian businesspeople. He was sharing how he got started in business and how he had always been driven to succeed at whatever he was doing. He began as a teenager, going door-to-door, selling products, which has to be one of the toughest jobs that there is. He became successful at it and was with the same company for some 20 years. He was not just successful at doing his job, but he was able to reach a lot of people's lives through his effort. At one point in this job, he was on the road around 240 days a year. He said that was fine when he was single, not so fine when he was married, and really tough when he became a parent.

If you find yourself relating to this because you have traveled a lot, or because you work a ton of hours at your job/ministry (pastors, this includes you), then I want you to be prepared for the statement that came from this man's wife to him:

"I don't know what you are called to do, but I doubt it is to fail as a husband or as a father."

If that does not rattle your cage, then you either have your life very well put-together, or you just don't get it at all. It rattles my cage on a number of levels personally:

Because of my calling to our family business, and in order to hopefully be financially successful, I too traveled a bit when our kids were very young. Not anywhere near 240 days a year, but enough to be an Alaska Airlines Gold Member. My wife was often left by herself to raise our three kids, and I want you to know that she did an awesome job of doing that! But I was blinded a bit, due to my lack of participation.

I also was so committed to working at our winery a couple of years ago that I worked 100 straight days. Many of these days were during the summer, which, as it turned out, was the last summer that all of my kids (with two in college) would be home together. Not at all my finest hour.

And finally, just this last year, in the middle of my year-long search for a paying job, one of my kids wrote to me, "we are so glad that you get to share your heart each week with people when you write, but Dad, the family is freaking out in financial insecurity, and so would you please increase your efforts to get out there and get a job? You've always told us any job is OK to do, to bring in some income." Now, mind you, writing something each week did not keep me from looking for work, and it was not my choice to go through such a drought. But I heard what was being said, and I probably won't ever forget it.

So I want to encourage everyone to hear what was said by this man's wife. And if I can try and define "callings," I would say that people may have many callings. You can be called to be a husband or wife, and you can be called to be a parent. You may have a calling to be a writer, to serve in ministry, or to just make a positive impact in your job. And because we can be living out multiple callings at the same time, I would like us to think hard about our lives. I would like us to ask ourselves, is there the possibility we might be failing at a calling or two? This is especially true when we get tunnel-vision to succeed at something or when we may feel that to be more spiritual, we have to sacrifice others in the process.

Now Jesus is clear that He is to be number one in our lives and our service to Him foremost in what we do. But I also believe that Jesus sees my calling to my family as part of his whole plan. And I really don't want this whole message to be about not neglecting our callings to our spouses and family (though I know that message will undoubtedly speak the loudest to most people), so I would like to highlight one other calling which I think is critical for everyone:

To participate in your community. Let me clarify right away that I am defining community in this reference as, the people with whom you are making some continuous contact. These are friends and acquaintances who rely on your presence and participation, just as your family relies on you, but obviously on a little different scale.

One thing I that I have learned from going through the long process of looking for a job is the value of relying on others in a community. And from my experience, I feel that I have a better grasp of what others need during their own periods of struggling. I have learned a bit of what it is like to be that person for others. And to do so, I must be present, I must participate with them. So I encourage all of you to use your experiences in life to be that person for others.

Sometimes it is just the simple matter of being present and participating; just being who you are makes an impact that you don't even know about. For the last couple of years, I have been having breakfast every Wednesday morning with the same guys at the same restaurant, and the serving staff at this restaurant has been the exact same as well, so we have developed a cordial bond with the staff. I have returned my gratitude for their hospitality to us by at times baking scones, muffins, or cookies and bringing them to the servers.

Now, over the last three weeks, I have worked morning shifts and have not been able to attend the Wednesday breakfast. I began to feel a longing for both my group and for our connection to the restaurant. So on my day off last Friday, I stopped by for a little bite to eat. In my time there, I was approached by five different staff members, all saying they had missed seeing me, and one of them brought a card, saying they had been holding onto it for the last few weeks. The note thanked me for all the treats I had brought in and for my uplifting spirit week after week. I had no idea of the impact of my participation in this community until I was spending time away from it.

There is a lot of information packed into this one writing, but my desire is that you will not miss what is at the heart of the message. I want to encourage you to be aware that you are called to live out several callings at one time and to be careful not to neglect of any of them. I also want you to be aware that there is great importance to your presence and participation in the lives of those you impact.

Are you aware?

I love this Moment. I loved the authenticity of my friend telling his story and how it hit so close to home for me. The rest of the writing just flowed from my heart.

A STRANGE PATH TO HOPE

02/28/2008

Therefore having been justified by faith, we have peace with God through our Lord Jesus Christ, through whom also we have obtained our introduction by faith into this grace in which we stand; and we exult in hope of the glory of God...

—Romans 5:1–2

These are very encouraging words from Paul. Faith, peace, grace, and hope in the glory of God certainly works for me. I can never get enough peace, I praise Him for all of his grace, and I am one that abounds in hope.

But then Paul goes on, and he kind of loses me in verses 3 and 4.

And not only this, but we also exult in our tribulations [I get that. James takes us down that thought path as well.], *knowing that tribulations bring about perseverance* [Sure, that's how that equation works. I am tracking so far.], *and perseverance, proven character* [I got this one too. We become better people after having gone down the perseverance road.], *and proven character, hope* [Whoa! Insert screeching halt noise and the smoking heels from a Flintstones' cartoon!].

Yes, for all you Bible scholars, I will get to verse 5, but I first want to figure out exactly how *hope* shows up here, right after gaining "proven character" from our tough times. The only way I see *hope* coming next in line is if I'm *hoping* I never go through that again.

Most of us have had our share of tribulations: our chances to obtain perseverance and claim a little proven character from the journey. But do you come out of that wearing a badge of hope? It's hard to see where the hope is going to come from when you are waiting for spiritual bruises to heal and for that proven character to show up.

Talk to people who have been incredibly wounded from a broken family. They wake up and just try to get through the day. Maybe hope is all they have to have to get through to the next day. Hope is how we survive the whole tribulation-filled journey. Hope really is pretty awesome, as Paul tells us when we finally read verse 5 in our Romans passage:

And hope does not disappoint, because the love of God has been poured out within our hearts through the Holy Spirit that was given to us.

God promises you hope! No matter where you are in a particular journey, be it in the middle of the initial tribulation, hanging on to perseverance, or finally seeing the proven character that comes forth, hope is coming!

It may be a strange path, but hope is coming and it does not disappoint. Praise God for that!

Sometimes the simplest statements are the best. This is by far the shortest Moment, and I had forgotten that I had ever written so few words. But as part of the journey in life this is one that is a constant companion to me. It may not have taken long to read this, but I know that you will be able to sit down with a group of people and spend a good deal of time with it.

JOURNEY

09/18/2008

I want to use this Wind-Fire Moment to reach out and encourage all who are currently working through tough times. Such times can take someone and make him or her very weary. We each carry our own wounds, fears, and trials. So I share with you this writing of mine that I penned during a quiet time with God and had appropriately called "Journey":

How can I completely let go
And not be so afraid of falling
How can I keep some control?

I often think I have my sights finally cleared
Only to find another hurdle is in my way
Sometimes I think I deserve much better than this

It is when I just can't see where there is to go
That I cry out to You for just a view
Lead me down Your winding road, Lord
I pray, "Give me just a moment in time,
So that I can rest in Your joy"

I never doubt You
I only doubt me

The night is always the darkest
I awake to find my doubts suffocating my thoughts
I must find You in this moment so that I will have peace

I never doubt You
I only doubt me

But today I stepped outside to a new morning's mist
There was such a change that was in the air
Like a rainbow, a promise of a clearing that was coming
Thank you for this moment that maybe only I could see

You have given me this moment and I am revived
I can now see that next step to take
I have been given the strength and I have found that joy
I have decided to let go

I know that many of you are hurting in some way. I know that many of you often feel lost and alone even though you are in the midst of everything and everyone. I know that doubts and fears can be overwhelming at times, but you still try to present that strong face. To all of you, I just want to say, it's alright. I want to tell you that you are not alone in struggling and that you are not without hope. I repeat: you are not alone! The devil would like us to think that we are alone, that no one else is struggling like we are, and most importantly, to feel that God must have abandoned us.

You're not alone for I am here
Let Me wipe away your every fear
My love I've never left your side
I have seen you through the darkest nights
And I'm the one who's loved you all your life
All of your life

—"You're Not Alone" by Meredith Andrews

I want to encourage everyone to do two things when you find yourself going through a challenging time:

Find that God is in the situation. We need to be confident in the fact that God is in the situation. He has to be, for if He was not, we would be without the hope that will see us through. Just because He has to be in it, does not mean that we will always see it right away. But His promise is to always be there, and in that we must hold our trust. Be diligent in your prayer, stand by your faith, and also let the vision of others help you to find Him.

Let go and give Him all the control. After flailing away and trying to solve the problem or to rescue ourselves, we find that the only power we have left is to finally let go completely. This is not permission to do nothing and just sit by and wait for God. He expects more from us than that. And it is also not a license to pick and choose the things that you are going to give up control of. This is a call for total surrender of everything to Him. When you let go of holding on to the situation, you have freed up your arms to hold on tightly to God. In this moment, He is free to guide you on the path to a resolution.

You may not currently be struggling with pain or fears (and if that is the case, then praise God that He has you in a good place), but I am very sure that you know someone who is. And my encouragement goes out to you as well. You need to be part of God's solution for that person, to make a difference in his or her life. We need to learn to be simple encouragers of others, and in that process we can also be ones who help to bring strength and healing.

And I also want to remind those of you who are in the midst of struggles: you can still be a witness to others, and you can still be an encouragement to others. When you are in the midst of a trial yourself, you have a keen sensitivity to what others are going through and are able to speak with an empathy that can reach deep down, past barriers that others may have put up. What better way to help yourself deal with a tough segment of life than to reach out to help others in their time of need?

This is another Moment that many people put on their lists for writings that they thought should be put into the book. But I do have to admit that it had been so long since the writing that I had to ask one of my daughters if she had written the "Journey" piece at the beginning. She writes a lot of poems and songs, so I thought that maybe I'd gotten it from her. But then we saw a couple of phrases that had too much of my signature on them.

Emotional Limbo

10/21/2010

Right now, my heart is kind of in limbo. I am going through a job application process, and have just finished level three of what appears to be a four-step process (with the final two or three candidates coming in for one last interview). I have been told that someone will circle back with me in the next couple of weeks. Ugh! It has been 10 months of being without a paying job. I would truly love to get this current possibility, but recent history has caused me to temper my heart's emotions on it. It leaves me in a place where I do not want to let myself channel deep emotional lows or skip along in praise and joy.

Have you ever been in this sort of emotional limbo? A place where your feelings won't seem to move up or down on the emotion Richter scale, or you just don't want them to? Have you been in a moment of time when you are emotionally motionless?

Believe me, if I were to get another call saying that this company was choosing to hire someone else, I could draw up the emotions to write a "Show me your scars" Wind-Fire Moment about how we may not truly find faith without going through pain that brings about total surrender to God. Conversely, if I were to suddenly be offered the job, I am sure that I would go around singing the Hallelujah Chorus.

I would love to stand up in this moment and claim Matthew 21:21–22:

And Jesus answered and said to them, "Truly I say to you, if you have faith, and do not doubt, you shall not only do what was done to the fig tree, but even if you say to this mountain, 'Be taken up and cast into the sea', it shall happen.

"And all things you ask in prayer, believing, you shall receive."

Whew! Come on now, "Pray it and claim it, and watch it happen." Sounds good, and I am sure that someone has written a book about that. But how do we really handle these verses? What do we do when we pray for months that a loved one would be healed of cancer, and then it doesn't happen? Did we not believe hard enough? What about praying for that next job, even over months and months and months? When a new job doesn't appear, does that mean we did not really believe when we prayed? Was there doubt that crept in?

I don't know if we truly have the answers to those questions. At least, I don't. But I do want to encourage you to spend some time with God, thinking deeply about it. If you are stuck in some land of emotional limbo, then I want to send a charge into your emotional life.

I know that my own thoughts make me take a hard look at those verses from Matthew. Do I believe that I could move a mountain with my faith? If that is what God wanted to happen, yes, I believe that is possible in some way. Do I ever have any doubt when I pray? Sure. I sometimes wonder if something is in God's will or if it is something that He is just leaving to be what it is.

Yet I carry on in a faith that will not waver. I carry on with a hope that is unsinkable. Which brings me to a verse that I have been struggling with as of late: "But now abide faith, hope, love, these three, but the greatest of these is love" (1 Corinthians 13:13).

I have been living through these trying times with such a tight grip on faith and hope, that I wondered how love could be still greater than those two. It seemed to me that what I really needed most to survive was to have my faith and my hope. I thought that I could truly love Him, but if I did not truly have faith and hope in Him to take care of me, that the feelings of love would not be enough to get me through.

But as I put it all together, with the help from these verses here, it started becoming clearer to me. What is it that I have no doubt about, that I fully believe in? That God promises to always love me.

I have no doubt that He loves me and that He is a God who heals the broken-hearted and that He will always take care of me. While I know His promise is not to keep me out of peril and tough times, I know that He will never leave or forsake me—because He passionately loves me!

Love really is the greatest of these. It is the love of the Father for me that I must hold onto. It is one thing I know I can count on in all instances. Love is the fuel to my faith and hope. And so, when I ask for these things in prayer, I am believing that God loves me, and I am fully confidant in receiving whatever will be allowed in His will.

What I have come to realize as I am writing the epilogues to each of these writings is how the Moments that dealt with our personal journeys being tough roads spoke to so many people. And talking about being in an emotional limbo was no different. The number of people who were currently going through their own limbo, or who had previously dealt with it were many.

DARKNESS

11/06/2008

What are three of the coolest things that come about on a dark, dark night? While snuggling into a warm, comfy bed after an exhausting day is a pleasure, that's not where I am going here. I think the three coolest things are:

1. A bright full moon, whether it is a yellow-orange Harvest Moon or one that is so piercingly clear and bright it reflects a river of light over a body of water.

2. The canvas sky filled with stars as far as the eye can see and too numerous to count. In Washington, sometimes the pleasure is just that we got a clear sky at all.

3. Lightning bolts. I mean, how cool is it when they light up the entire sky and you get to see the lightning's jagged veins scattering about!

All three of these best things about a dark night are actually sources of light, made even brighter by the darkness that surrounds them. You see, in times of darkness we are always drawn to the light.

Darkness, which by definition is the absence of light, can often be a very overwhelming presence. Physical darkness can put fear in us, and spiritual darkness can weigh down our souls and make us fearful as well, whether it is the great evil that is often described as darkness in the Bible, or our own actions that are the product of this absence of spiritual light.

My kids will tell you that my motto is, "bad things happen after 2 a.m." There is nothing about 2 a.m. that is significant, but it seems that every time you read about someone being shot, or driving their car off a road, it happens in the deep night after 2 a.m. Now that doesn't mean I don't want them to be up that late, but they know it is not a time that I want them out without purpose. It is not what they will do but the actions of others around them, that they have no control over, that I worry about.

There is something about the darkness that draws things amiss, creates an avenue for depression to heighten and for evil to flourish. Why do you think bars and lounges are so often kept dark, even in the middle of a day? They are places people go to to forget the reality of their situation and to avoid the light that would reveal their actions.

My encouragement to you here is two-fold. First, it is to encourage you to avoid the trappings of darkness, and second, it is to inspire you to likewise encourage others who are dealing with bad personal choices or struggling with a spiritual darkness that is the absence of God's presence.

I want to focus on two elements of darkness as well. One is actions we should avoid that lead to darkness, and the other is the emotional depths we often feel inside that darkness.

"Do not participate in the unfruitful deeds of darkness, but instead even expose them."   — Ephesians 5:11

It is easy enough to say, just don't do evil, but often we have emotional investments in actions we know to be wrong. And, as Paul says in Romans, we do what we do not want to do. I had a friend who shared with me about his struggle with pornography while he traveled. He made some efforts to overcome this, such as asking the hotel to turn of the channels in his room that offered those shows, but sometimes the hotel would forget to do it and he would stumble again. You see, he was looking to some earthly solution, to another human being, to avoid the darkness, instead of turning to the light.

Instead of trying desperately to keep temptation out of the room and thereby focusing even more on the darkness, my friend needed to turn towards God's light. He could have done something as simple as turning on some worship music instead of the TV, committing to opening up his Bible whenever the urge hit, or just going to his knees in prayer to invite the light into the room. With an addiction like pornography, the enemy had told him that he needed or even deserved these emotional pleasures. The darkness may not always be as simple to combat as I describe, but we must work to replace the voices in the darkness with the Voice of the light.

Flooding light into the darkness is our only hope!

"The night is almost gone, and the day is at hand. Let us lay aside the deeds of darkness, and put on the armor of the light."

—Romans 13:12

And finally, there is emotional darkness. The enemy thrives in the darkness because he knows this is where we are weak and feel most alone. These emotional depths definitely intensify during the dark times of the night, when an emotionally and physically draining day combines with despair to create a darkness that covers our vision of a path to hope.

It is through this time that people need encouragement and support, because it is at this time that we question whether a path exists to take us out of the darkness. I often find this to be very true in my own spiritual life. But the hope that I have found, and the I lesson that I have learned, is that when times are at their darkest, it is then that I see Him most clearly. That is the time when His light will shine most brightly.

"Do not rejoice over me, O my enemies; though I will fall I will arise; though I dwell in darkness, the Lord is a light to me."   —Micah 7:8

Seek to take the Light with you wherever you go. This way you will be able to navigate your way through darkness and to reflect His light into the life of others.

"Your words are exactly what I needed to hear... 'Flooding light into the darkness is our only hope!' This will be my new mantra." This was one of the responses that came to this Moment. Another person responded, "Last Wednesday (my husband) found out that he is being laid off from his job—it's easy to go down the road of thinking worst-case scenarios (your words were, letting darkness cover the path of hope). Instead we need to flood the light!"

Once again, stories of struggle on the "Journey" hit close to where people are.

THE SCARS

12/16/2010

Complete: *thorough; entire; total; undivided, uncompromised, or unmodified.*

Surrender: *to yield or relinquish possession or power; to resign in favor of another.*

Completely surrendering your life to God can bring about the most intimate of relationships with Him. I have my doubts as to whether it is possible to appreciate the richness of a deep and passionate relationship with the Lord unless you have received the scars of having been brought to a place when you have let go because there is nothing else left for you to hold onto.

Until circumstances have brought you to that point in your faith, where you have nothing of your own understanding and power left to cling to, will you ever make that uncompromised relinquishment of your will to God?

And there is a difference from thinking it is a good idea to let go and having to do so. It is a place where you are no longer wondering how you will make it through the next week, month, or year, but how you might even take your very next step. It is a place where your heart cries out to God to deliver to you His peace and understanding, for you will never be able sustain your journey yourself.

A variety of things can bring a person to this point. It could be going through an extreme illness, divorce or marriage struggles, the death of a child or spouse, or long, drawn-out financial stress: something that strips away all of your earthly abilities to handle or resolve it. These are the times when we must let go and see the richness of relationship that is there to be had with God. In these times I want to encourage you:

To find great peace in the midst of struggle. I have been amazed at how fast (immediately) God's peace can come when we call for Him out of surrender. Even while your circumstances stay the same, God delivers a peace that surpasses all understanding.

I feel this peace in no way better than in my ability to go to bed at night and fall asleep without fear or anxiety. I have slept far better through what have been my greatest times of struggle than at any time before, when things were not at such a level of uncertainty. This is because all I would allow myself to focus on was God, because I could no longer figure anything out myself. So I would ask God to take away all fear and regrets, and to not allow them to seep into my thoughts. It would be just me and Him.

To find other strengths and your destiny. As I listened to my friend Jim speak to a group of people last week about finding your destiny, it struck me that, even though I was back to work, and at a job that might be a wonderful next career, I felt that at this time in my life, work was a means to an end and maybe not really what God has for me as a destiny.

But during my walk through the jungle (which is far from over), God has brought me into the writing of the Wind-Fire Moment every week, and the creation of the community which is the Third Thursday Bistro. Both of which I fully believe to be part of God's chosen destinies for this time of my life.

So I encourage you to look for destinies that may lie outside of the workplace or home life. It could be places where you have found some personal strength that may not have been so visible before.

To hear clearly and to keep hope alive. When you have completely surrendered and you are reliant on God alone, it is amazing how you are able to hear from Him and to feel His presence when all around you appears to be turmoil. There is an understanding delivered by the Holy Spirit that tells you that you will be OK, and tells your heart how you will proceed.

People have often come to me and expressed amazement at how calmly I have related the story of my circumstances. It was because at times there was no other choice for me but to surrender to Him and walk in His peace, having faith that things would get better. And in doing so, it allowed me to hold onto any dreams that I might have had.

As I was preparing to write this, I was listening to a song from *Child of the Promise*, a musical about the Christmas story. This song is sung by Elizabeth. I have learned to love the mother of John the Baptist and the wife of Zacharias. Like Sarah in the Old Testament, she is older and has pretty much given up hope of ever having a child. She has resigned herself to being a woman of ridicule and disgrace in the community because of her lack of being able to conceive. She has her scars. But then God moves. The song shows the hope born through the scars:

> *Isn't it just like the Lord to invite me to put all my dreams in His hands;*
> *Forever releasing the grips that once held them, forever surrendering my plans:*
>
> *And then when He's certain it's not born of men,*
> *He calls for the fire to rekindle again*
>
> *And He asks me to know in my heart*
> *What's not seen with my eyes;*
> *So the dream never dies...*

So my hope is that you will find something in your life that convinces you to completely surrender to your Savior. And hopefully, you will not have to go to a great depth of struggle to find the depth of richness that will come from uncompromised yielding of your life to Him. A steadfast faith that allows your hope to live on is truly wonderful!

I was asked by someone who heads up a job-transition group if he could share this one with the people in that group. And a very good friend said that he could completely relate to the message, and it reminded him of how his own surrender had helped him navigate through brain cancer.

WALK STRAIGHT THROUGH

02/19/2009

The forest of life is very thick this week; the darkness keeps shouting at me. Someone shared with me one man's observation of a personal struggle as "walking straight through the middle of a tar pit," and I have to say, it's been that kind of week. I have heard the enemy throughout, sending his demons to taunt me with lies. All of the proverbial windows for God to open seemed to be stuck shut. But an interesting and sadly comforting thing about this week is, no matter how thick the forest seems or how long as this tunnel of darkness appears to be, I keep running into a lot of other people there. This is a time when many are facing some tough battles of all kinds.

But through it all, I am finding that, for one of the first times in my life, I know that I am going to be better off if I just walk straight into the middle of everything. I must face things head-on and head straight into the battle. No more avoiding that which will ultimately come later. No more veering off to the left and then back to the right, just to stay out of the thicket. No more taking a few small steps forward to find that it only ends up taking me giant leaps back.

It's time to grab the sword of William Wallace and attack the thicket. It's time to catch a lightsaber tossed from a fellow Jedi Knight and to go right after the demons that continue to speak lies to me. I must run into the battle. I must not fear. But I will not run alone!

Hallelujah! Salvation and glory and power belong to our God.
—Revelation 19:1

"Hallelujah! For the blood of the Lamb that was slain. And so we enter in to see Your face, oh God" ("Hallelujah" by Tenth Avenue North).

Hallelujah! I will find comfort and rest under His Wings.

Hallelujah! I know that there are those who love me and will stand by me, risking injury themselves, until the battle ends.

Hallelujah! I am His, and He will never leave me.

Hallelujah! I can often see the red sky at night that promises me a hope for a better tomorrow ("Red Sky" by Brandon Heath).

...and though you do not see Him now, but believe in Him, you greatly rejoice with joy inexpressible and full of glory. —1 Peter 1:8

Hallelujah! You always pick me up off the ground.

Hallelujah! I find a way to dance and to sing Your praise.

Hallelujah! For the Lord our God, the Almighty, reigns.

—Revelation 19:6

Hallelujah! Though I may be blind to my future path, I believe in that which the human eye cannot see.

Hallelujah! My heart beats strong even after it takes a beating.

Hallelujah! I will not let the enemy derail me from the path the Lord has set forth for my heart. I will swing the sword and march forward and rejoice!

Rejoice in the Lord always, again I will say rejoice.

—Philippians 4:4

I know that I will most likely not be miraculously removed from the dense jungle, nor will the tar pit suddenly disappear. But I know that I will make it through them. My encouragement to everyone is that, whether you are struggling through this jungle or one of those that the rest of us will rely on to help us through, there is something for you to be doing.

If you are facing the jungle, I want to encourage you to grab your lightsaber and head straight in. Pick up the fight and move onward and upward.

And I want to encourage you to be ready to fight for someone else. You may be the one who will help to free that person from being stuck and going nowhere. I encourage you to walk along with them for a while by offering your strength, so that they may find some recuperation and thus be much stronger to move forward.

There is no need for anyone to ever fell like they are doing this alone!
Satisfy me, Lord
I'm begging you to help me see
You're all I want, You're all I need
Satisfy me, Lord
Your love is all I need to live

—*"Satisfy" by Tenth Avenue North*

Not only did this writing inspire a lot of people to ask how they could be praying for me, which was a wonderful thing, but there were many great comments:

"Wow, this is how I feel many times—pushing through the darkness, asking the Lord to give the faith I don't have on my own, and I bump into others along the same path, sharing their journey and being surprisingly blessed on such a dark path! We humans are so weak and finite, and our Lord God is so infinite, limitless, indescribable!"

A pastor friend said that he would be forwarding it to several people that week.

"Love the part about fighting for someone else... we are not alone."

—SECTION FIVE—

COMMUNITY

Community has become an indispensible aspect of my faith. Everyone is looking for true community in their lives, but we all seem to have trouble finding it. The following Wind-Fire Moments are about different aspects of community: serving others, being faithful, or just being a friend.

One of them talks about a place called the Third Thursday Bistro. As you will read, this is a once-a-month evening that began as inspiration to open up a spot where people could just stop by and have a place to come gather and to enjoy a little food and wine, and not have it cost them anything. It would be a place of authentic fellowship and a little sanctuary. But then God took over as only He can.

I believe that the need for this kind of place could in itself be the subject of a whole chapter or book. In fact, the type of place is found in theory in a fiction book called *Bo's Café*, a book that is well worth reading. The Third Thursday Bistro shows that when you are obedient to following God's calling to your heart, that God is faithful to reveal opportunities that you never would have dreamed of.

COMMUNITY

01/27/2011

Every time that I write a Wind-Fire Moment that touches on an aspect of community, I get a number of responses telling me that community is an issue that is on their hearts and they always like to hear about it. I love getting their encouragement, but it makes me wonder: why is community such a hard thing to come by these days?

As I often do, I went to Dictionary.com to look up the definition of the word in question. What I found said that community is "a social group sharing common characteristics or interests... perceiving itself as distinct in some respect from the larger society." That is a good and broad definition to start with. This kind of community can be found in many places: at churches, Bible studies, men's/women's groups, social clubs, schools, neighborhoods, or sometimes (though not often) in the workplace.

Why then is community so hard to find for many of us? Every time I ask this question of people, I hear the same few things are missing: leadership, time, and vision.

Leadership. I am surprised how often people mention leadership as something needed for community. They don't mean a leader in the political sense, but one who helps to tie things together and keep a vision on track. I think of a head pastor; the pastor is the one who continues to put out the message that says what sort of community is going to be found in his church. Similarly, a small city or town council says what type of community their town will be, and people can decide to live there, comfortable that they know what type of community they will be living in.

Time. Why is there so little community in the neighborhoods in which we live? Maybe because we all get up and drive 45 minutes to our place of work to hang out with everyone else who just drove 45 minutes from a different direction. Then, tired and dragging, we all return to our homes and hunker down inside with family. And churches, in their attempt to accommodate people's busy schedules (and sometimes due to their size), have three or four service times, scattering the community. Thus, churches have small life/home fellowship groups to allow people the chance to find some intimate community.

Vision/Common thread. Common interest and motivation bonds people into a community, making it distinct from the larger society. It is the vision that will help to motivate people to want to participate in what is going on and also help to carry them through the tough times. And again highlighting the importance of leadership, when someone will champion this focus, the vision retains strength and momentum, and people have something to hold onto. Even the best of symphonies and choirs need a director up front to keep them all on the same beat.

Now that we know the components of a good community, what does it take to get one in place? Let's look at one experience I know well: the monthly gathering I have been hosting/facilitating for the last couple of years called Third Thursday Bistro (TTB). One night a month, I go to the Estate House at the winery, cook some food, pour some wine, and open the doors to anyone who wants to show up. This unique gathering has prompted a number of the comments on community and how it is not very commonplace in our culture.

I have been told that the TTB has worked because of my commitment as a *leader* to be there every month. I was the one who spent the money at the beginning to buy all the food and initiated the group by letting people know it existed. You see, TTB has no official invitation, no RSVPs; people are just made aware of it, and the Spirit leads from there. I know full well that it is God's evening, and He has allowed me to facilitate with a gracious excitement, if you will, to welcome anyone.

My excitement as host is a combination of my mother's tremendous heart of hospitality and my father's enjoyment of experiencing people. I received good training by traveling with my father when I was growing up. We could be in any city, stop in any place, and my dad would start up a conversation with someone he didn't know. If they were locals, we would talk about where we were, and if they were visitors like us, we found out all about where they were from. By the time we left, we always knew their names and what interested them. In this way, my dad made community wherever went.

The Third Thursday Bistro also works because of its *time*. It's only one time a month, but it is consistent: same day and same place each month. Not everyone can make it every month, but acceptance is not based on consistent attendance. The format is not strict. You can come every week or only once. There is no time you have to be there by, and you can stop in for 10 minutes or three hours. It is whatever you need it to be.

And yes, we have a common **vision**, a little distinction that this is something different from what is going on anywhere else. We're people who enjoy sharing good food and wine. And then there is the fellowship that we share every month, which I believe is the deep essence of TTB that continues to draw people back time and again and encourages them to invite others to come and experience the special community they have found.

I hear many stories from friends about how God has allowed them to find refuge, relaxation, and a place to connect in these evenings. Some of the best comments come from new people, saying they were a little hesitant to show up because they just didn't quite understand the open, "come hang out with people you probably don't know, eat some food, and enjoy some wine if you like, nothing else happens, no requirements" nature of the evening. And then they leave saying, "Oh, now I get it. I hope I can make it again next month."

Is it unique? Yes. But maybe it is a little more the way God originally intended community to be.

It seems to be what people are really looking for.

The description of community here prompted someone to share these words with a pastor and with another pastor who lived half a country away, and both pastors shared them with their congregations. I do believe there is a concept of community here that people are hungry for.

I love sharing about the Third Thursday Bistro whenever I can and would love to help spread the word on this. I do know someone who just moved away that said they were thinking of trying to do something like it in their new town. They asked me if I would be OK with that. I thought it was a wonderful idea.

HELPING OUT

08/16/2007

I was driving to one of my son Michael's baseball games on a Sunday afternoon. As I started to make my way up a very long hill, I suddenly heard and felt something bounce underneath my car and apparently out the back. I hadn't seen anything coming at me. I immediately checked my temperature gauge, which fortunately wasn't racing up, but the smoke beginning to come out the back of my car was not a good sign.

I continued my way up the hill until I was able to pull off into the entrance of a neighborhood. It was a very large entrance to a fairly well-to-do community, so I pulled in and made my way over to the side of the road, safely out of the way.

I got out of the car, seeing a little smoke now coming out of the hood. As I made my way around the front, I looked down under the car to see some fluid coming out. It was oil, and it was flowing from my car. That noise from under my car was my oil plug.

Grateful I had my cell phone with me, I called AAA to come get the car, and then called my wife to come get me. It took an hour for the tow truck to come.

My Good Samaritan question for all of you is: How many people do you think took the time to stop and see if I needed anything during the hour that I sat there?

My wife's quick answer was, "Zero." My best friend said, "One." Megan, my assistant at the office, also said, "One." Sound about right?

The answer: *eight*. Yes, that is right. Improve your faith in your fellow man, everyone.

Someone who was behind me coming up the hill pulled in to see if I needed help and offered their cell phone, before I even had a chance to pull mine out.

Another person stopped when I was on the phone to AAA, asking if I needed a ride somewhere. A guy with the local city maintenance (or something like that) stopped to see if I needed help and to offer me a couple gallons of gas if that was the issue. One lady on her way out of the neighborhood offered me a cold bottle of water. She apologized that it was all she could offer at the moment because she was on her way out somewhere.

And one ironic stop was a guy heading out of the neighborhood with a kayak on the top of his car. I had heard him coming down the street because of some "clacking" noise coming from his car. As he pulled over to check out the noise, he felt obligated to ask if I was OK, which I was.

As he walked all the way around his car, apparently looking for the noise, I asked, "Looking for that clacking noise?"

"Yes, I am," he said.

"Well your strap on the other side over there is flopping and hitting the kayak." So there I was, waiting to be helped, and I was able to return all this good favor. by helping someone else.

I want to encourage you to look at the example that Jesus set for us. Take the time to look at who it was that Jesus was always helping out. Were they only the people who lived on His road or only those who went to the same synagogue He attended? No! How about the crippled man at the pool of Bethesda? Never met him before. The centurion's servant, the official's son, the paralytic lowered in from the roof, any one of the blind people, or the woman who touched his tunic? Jesus didn't know them either. The list goes on and on. And who doesn't love the story of the woman at the well? He reached out to those in need and to those whom God presented to Him.

I love that about Jesus. It didn't matter who it was, where they were from, what they could offer Him, or what they had done. I try to tell this idea to young people I share with. There are so many kids at a junior or senior high school that have run out of emotional gas. They have broken down on the side of the road. Does anyone stop and see if they need anything, even just offer a smile and "How are you doing?" It doesn't matter if they are in your group of friends or not. And it certainly doesn't matter if they are in the "cool" group or not.

How are you doing in this area? Ask God to point out when there is someone that you need to help out or encourage. Maybe it is someone you don't currently know. More likely, it is someone you do know, whose needs are going unrecognized. We are to be the "salt of the earth" and the "protectors of the light" are we not?

The group Casting Crowns has a wonderful song called "Does Anybody Hear Her" that asks Christians: are we really seeing others and the situations that they are in, or are we too busy judging them to see what their hearts really need?

She is yearning for shelter and affection
That she never found at home
She is searching for a hero to ride in
To ride in and save the day
And in walks her prince charming
And he knows just what to say
Momentary lapse of reason and she gives herself away...

Does anybody hear her? Does anybody see?
Or does anybody even know she's going down today
Under the shadow of our steeple
With all the lost and lonely people
Searching for the hope that's tucked away in you and me
Does anybody hear her? Does anybody see?

If judgment looms under every steeple
If lofty glances from lofty people
Can't see past her scarlet letter
And we never even met her...

Just the week after this event with my car, I was on my way to work when I saw a guy attempting to push his stalled car off the main road and back onto the street he had just entered from. Cars were whizzing on by him...

Of course, I stopped.

This was the very first Wind-Fire Moment that I wrote following my introduction message, and it has always been one of my very favorites. In some ways, it is at the origin of my passion for community and why I have such a heart for it. It is a message that is timeless. And if you were like my wife and the others as you read this, and were surprised at how many people stopped, then I hope that your heart for community will have gained a little inspiration.

Semper Fidelis

06/17/2010

If you are a fan of the TV show *NCIS* like my kids and I, you will know that *Semper Fidelis*, Latin for "always faithful," is the motto of the US Marines. Marines often say *Semper Fi* to one another, whether they have served together or have just met. It's a kind of shorthand for saying, "I have your back, and I know that you have mine. I will carry faith in you and what we are doing, until the day you prove otherwise." It says, "I will give my life for you." It is the code of the Corps to be trustworthy.

I love this attitude! When I was talking about this at my Wednesday morning breakfast, my good friend called it "the baseline of true community." No wonder I love the idea.

Let a man regard us in this manner, as servants of Christ, and stewards of the mysteries of God. In this case, moreover, it is required of stewards to be found trustworthy. —I Corinthians 4:1–2

This inspires me, and I hope that it inspires you. It makes me wonder, though, if Christians really behave with this sort of conviction to always be faithful to each other while living in community. I fear it is not so. I know that the time we share with each other often does not involve life-and-death situations, as it does in the military. Yet in truth the lives that we share with each other are centered in the midst of a most intense spiritual battle where, at the very least, our actions could be a contributing factor to a fellow believer being left "wounded in action."

Where is our belief in the Christian *Semper Fi*? Is this a common core value to the church/fellowship structure? My first response again would be to say no.

If your church has this going, then I stand corrected and I applaud you. But if this exists, I have the feeling it is very few and far between.

I understand that is the purpose of many of the small group programs that are the current trend in churches. The "life groups" that many churches offer brings intimacy in community for people within a large congregation. And the "Band of Brothers" theme is patterned after the idea of a small military platoon of trustworthy men to help each other get through their spiritual battles. I also understand that small groups are the only way to develop intimate allies, people to whom we have greater responsibility and whom we know on a deeper level. And in the best of scenarios, that is what happens within those groups.

But what I want to see is a prevailing attitude that would carry across the board, an attitude that is worn at all times, that says, "Fellow believer, you can trust me to care about you, and trust that I am always ready." And whether you are a believer today or not, it says, "I am there to uphold my commitment to care about the fact that your heart matters to God as well, and I will protect and serve you in that way."

That is what I like about the Marines: you don't have to be in my platoon for *Semper Fidelis* to be in place. You just have to be a Marine. And their commitment to sacrifice is not just limited to protecting other Marines; it is for all the people that they serve. I fear that the Christian community does not have a strong reputation outside of its own walls to serve in this way and with this passion.

People are alone out there. People are hurting. And people are caught in stagnant places in their faiths. They need their neighbors to be "always faithful," and it is my encouragement to us to live this way.

The hurting goes deep within the Christian community today, and it requires a commitment on all our parts to live out *Semper Fidelis*, especially with the Christians out there who are very alone with themselves. Even when they are attending a church or spending time in groups within business meetings, people can still feel that way inside. There is a great line from a song called "Sun-Stars-Moon" by the Paul Colman Trio:

"I'm a lonely soul... when I think I'm alone"

See? It just takes one of us to think, "I am alone," to be lonely. This is where the Christian *Semper Fi* must come into play. And one key area of being faithful is by putting action to our words. In this day and age, it is so easy to come into contact with and to communicate with a lot of different people, and it is even easier to toss around some of our "catch you later" lines:

"I should call you sometime."

"I will pray for you."

"We should get together soon."

I want to encourage us to be critical of all the things we might say in passing. We may say them with good intention, but then we move on with our too-busy lives without realizing that someone out there may have a real need and might have grabbed onto your gesture. Maybe these are people who really need others praying for them, or they just need a friend to actually call (or write) back to them. *They need someone to be faithful to them.* And when someone does not follow up with them, *Semper Fidelis* is broken, and our brothers and sisters are left wounded.

There is great power in our words, and we need to stay faithful to the commitments that we make when using them.

My encouragement to you is to always be faithful to the calling that God has for you and to live out your life in actions that honor Him and are true to others. We can't just choose to put it aside when we want to. There is just too much at stake!

Semper Fi, my brothers and sisters!

The responses came flowing in after this one. People found it convicting and were led to contact other people. One woman sent it along to her brother, who was ex-Navy and a new believer.

One person was inspired by the "accountability" aspect and commented that even when he feels he has earned someone's trust and respect, he still rarely finds a welcome reaction when he challenges someone with correction. He said there is a need in correcting others to be gentle but not a wimp. And this message was a reminder not to retreat from a brother but to be direct in fellowship.

Another felt that 99 percent of people don't do it, and still another was reminded to get a note of encouragement off to someone and was "doing it next."

THE HYPOTHETICAL

04/28/2011

What if?

What if you won the Lottery tomorrow? Would you still go to work?

What if you knew that you only had six months to live? Would you live your life any differently?

I want to play the game with you. But these will not be your standard hypothetical questions. These are questions I want to stir your heart with. I want to encourage us to look at the duty we have to reach out to the world, but also to see that we need to be able to receive the world.

What if someone were hurting? Whether that hurt was emotional, physical, or financial, would that person come to you to find guidance, understanding, or healing?

Would that person see you as someone who would be able to listen to his or her story and as a safe place to speak?

We need to be so authentic with our lives that people will see that we hurt and that we have struggles just like anyone else. We should not hide behind the Christian veil that "all is well." We are not perfect and should never pretend to be.

I love the fact that people came to find Jesus when they were broken and hurting. We may not have His ability to heal people physically, but if we are to be Christ-like, then we should believe that the Holy Spirit will provide us what we need to help people with their situations.

The question again is, "would someone come to you?" Would they go to your church and not feel as though they were the only one struggling?

What if someone were seeking the truth and were not sure that God really existed? Would they want to talk to you? And if they did, would they end up seeing a God that they wanted to know more about?

I worry that sometimes believers rush to put the "Christian sleeper-hold" on someone who is lost and seeking. A litany of Christian-speak to someone who has no basis for that vocabulary will never get that person to the place of an intimate relationship with God.

Are we real enough that people would have the desire to be around us? Are we able to hold a relationship with a non-believer without trying to convert him or her at every turn?

As believers we should never have to compromise any of our beliefs to attract the attention of others. In fact, the opposite is true. By living as a reflection of the One who made us, we offer up a space that is safe for someone to come as they search.

I always come back to the woman at the well. Jesus did not chase the woman away by condemning her lifestyle or telling her about the seven steps to becoming a Christian. Jesus spoke the truth about her life and about who He was. He spoke the truth about what He had to offer. He was truthful about who she was. And she was drawn to the truth.

What if someone who was living a life that could be considered misguided began to seek out some direction and counsel?

Would they find in you a condemning spirit? Or would they be able to stay around you long enough so that God could be the One to begin the work in their hearts?

Would they trust you? Think about the risk that someone might take to come and be real with you, to share something that might bring great judgment from the majority of Christians he or she knows.

I love the story of Jesus and the people getting ready to stone the woman for adultery. What a great picture of giving her new life, by saying that there is no one left to condemn her. He tells her to go and sin no more, but absence of sin was not a prerequisite for Him to save her.

How would the adulterous woman, or a girl who has taken up prostitution as a way to make a living, be received by you? Or what would she find in the church today? Would the church be free of condemnation, so that she might actually stay around long enough to find the love and compassion that Jesus offers freely?

My hope is that if you found yourself at all uncomfortable with these "what ifs," that you will find encouragement to make some evaluations of your approachability.

The people who needed Jesus the most always felt they could go to Him. They did not seem to worry about what He would think of them or if they were worthy of His love.

You have to love that about Jesus. This is all the reason more to set as our goal to be more like Him.

This one received many positive responses, especially from those that said it was so close to their heart. I always like when a pastor gives me positive feedback, especially when I deal with issues about Christians and their attitudes towards non-believers.

—SECTION SIX—

KNOWING GOD

I always hope that my writings will be focused on encouraging the hearts of others. I hope that they will allow you to see God more clearly and to be more aware of Him in your daily walk.

Each of these sections is powerful in its own way. But the eight reflections in this section will challenge you to define how you see God and encourage you to go deeper in your relationship with Him.

My prayer is that you will celebrate the intimate relationship that He is calling you into. And while much of this will not be anything that you have not heard or thought of before, I believe it will encourage you to go back to making it a constant part of your spiritual walk.

I AM

01/10/2008

At the end of Moses' encounter with God in the burning bush, Moses asks God,

"Behold I am going to the sons of Israel and I shall say to them, 'The God of your fathers has sent me to you.' Now they may say to me, 'What is his name?' What shall I tell them?"

And God said to Moses, "I AM WHO I AM."

—Exodus 3:13–14

Right... I would have to side with Moses on this one. I am going back to tell people that the God who has been silent for all these years has chosen to talk to me, and I get to tell them His name is, "I AM"? On the one hand, that is a very "studly" name. Sorry, Mom. (She never liked using the term "stud.") It is simple, right to the point, and nothing else needs to be added. It's no different, I guess, than how we parents like to get away with, "Because I said so," or, "Because I AM the parent." Simple, right to the point, and nothing else needs to be added.

Look at the words to the Mark Schultz song, "I AM," which is one of my favorites of all time. He had seen a poster at his church that listed all the names of God, and that inspired the lyrics for this song.

I AM the Maker of the Heavens
I AM the Bright and Morning Star
I AM the Breath of all Creation
Who always was
And is to come

I AM the One who walked on water
I AM the One who calmed the seas
I AM the Miracles and Wonders
So come and see
And follow Me
You will know

chorus:
I AM the Fount of Living Water
The Risen Son of Man
The Healer of the Broken
And when you cry
I AM your Savior and Redeemer
Who bore the sins of man
The Author and Perfecter
Beginning and the End
I AM

I AM the Spirit deep inside you
I AM the Word upon your heart
I AM the One who even knew you
Before your birth
Before you were

Before the Earth (I AM)
The universe (I AM)
In every heart (I AM)
Oh, where you are (I AM)
The Lord of Lords (I AM)
The King of Kings (I AM)
The Holy Lamb (I AM)
Above all things

So what does God really say to Moses when He says, "I AM WHO I AM"?
It is very clear to me now. God is saying:

I AM who you need me to be. I AM everything.

Isn't that the great thing about God? We all find something a little different about Him, because we all have so many different needs. We have all been created uniquely, and to have relationship with Him, so that must mean that He needs to be able to meet us where we are. And He does!

My encouragement to you is to spend some time looking at the words to this song and find the names and characteristics of God that apply to your life right now. You may find a name that is not even in the song. Then, spend some time thanking God for who He is. The very cool thing is that tomorrow, weeks from now, or next year, a different one of those names may meet you where you are. And in the past, it may have been something else entirely. God meets you where you are. HE IS WHO HE IS.

My heart always leaps when I hear in the song, "the healer of the broken and when you cry, I AM *your* Savior and Redeemer." I guess to me, that is where He meets me daily. I can get through my day with strength, energy, hope, and a spirit to encourage others, because there is a constant state of healing and redeeming going on in my life.

For those of you who have seen the movie *Terminator 2* or watched the TV show *Heroes*, you have seen characters who, no matter how badly they have been injured, automatically regenerate and become whole, without a scratch remaining. That is how I often feel my life must be. Though I know I carry a few scars, He heals me when I am hurt, and He redeems me when I fall. *He is* who I need Him to be.

Who is HE to you?

I wrote this one in less than an hour. That week I had an entirely different message ready to go, and on my way to work, I heard this song. The Holy Spirit put it on my heart: "Here is today's message."

The responses were awesome as people got back to me with who God is to them. If you are in a small group, this topic should generate a great discussion.

GOD MOMENTS

08/23/2007

Not too long ago, I read a story from a friend of mine about her encounter with a complete stranger on a bus to the Los Angeles airport. She was just finishing a trip where she had been looking for (and had yet to find) some direction from God about her family's plan to move back to L.A. After finding out that this man she had just met was a Christian, my friend told him about her situation and said, "You are my last hope for God to speak."

Yes, she actually said that. Then she gave him her name and phone number and said, if he knew of anyone wanting to rent a house to a Christian family for a year, to call her. He said, "I know someone who is going away for three years [this was actually the exact time her family would need a house]. I will give you his name."

My response to her story was that I would no longer run from crazy ladies that come and sit down next to me on public transportation.

"Ya callin' me crazy?" she replied. "*I just live looking for a God Moment.*"

I just love that statement! Don't you? Why aren't we all living our lives looking for God Moments?

I know that some of you are saying, "What does looking for a God Moment really mean?" You know, I think that answer will be different for everyone. Everyone's relationship with God is just a little different. So the things that are a God Moment for me might not connect with you. To me, it is a moment that only God could have orchestrated. And I believe that God has a complete symphony of moments for us all to find if we so desire.

For example:

When I drive to work and see the moon in the blue morning sky or Mount Rainier jumping out majestically, that is God telling me that He is here today, and "please enjoy." That is a God Moment to me. And believe me, I look for those every day. Or as I am driving, I look over and notice a dad walking with his kids, and I see that his almost teenage daughter is holding his hand as they walk. My heart is warmed because I see family, love, and security for those kids. Oh, that is such a God moment to me!

I pray each morning in my quiet time for God to give me a moment to encourage someone that day. It may come through a conversation, an e-mail, or a phone call, or in an encounter with a stranger. I pray that He will make my heart aware of whatever it is, when it happens. And when that time comes, I know it has been a God Moment. To my friend, it was that "no-way" chance that the last person she would talk to on her way to the airport, and a complete stranger at that, would have an answer to something she had been seeking the whole trip.

I love the book *The Sacred Romance* by John Eldredge. It changed my view of my personal relationship to God. It opened my eyes to a God who is passionate in His love for me and has a great desire to relate with me personally. It is why I was created. Now I am able to understand my God enough so that I can recognize His joy in the beauty of His creation, and His joy in seeing me living out the glory He has created me for. It taught me to look for and recognize God Moments.

What are your God Moments? Are you looking for them? They are out there. When you find one, take the time to share it with someone else. What a blessing it would be for them to hear from your heart!

I cannot believe that this was the third WFM that I wrote (counting The Intro week). That would make it some four years ago. And while it does not seem like just yesterday, I am shocked that it has been that long.

If this book is about anything, it is about finding God in everyday Moments, and this was such a perfect example of that. My hope is that if you do not have one of these stories to share with someone, that you will pray for the eyes of your heart to be able to see yourself in one.

WHAT DO I KNOW OF HOLY?

06/18/2009

Recently, I was searching and searching for inspiration. Then one day I woke up early to finish my thoughts for what was to be a Wind-Fire Moment for that week, and I was flooded that whole morning with ideas for other topics, ideas I felt I could just sit down and finish in one stroke.

It is really nice when the Spirit is so clear with His inspirations, and it is good to be in such a place that you just seem to see it all. But I convinced myself to stay the course and finish my original thought, mostly due to how much I am inspired by this particular song.

Whether or not you have ever heard the song "What Do I Know of Holy?" from the group Addison Road, the real question would be, have you ever really *heard* the words:

I made You promises a thousand times
I tried to hear from heaven
But I talked the whole time
I think I made You too small
I never feared You at all, no
If You touched my face, would I know You?
Looked into my eyes, could I behold You?

What do I know of You
Who spoke me into motion?
Where have I even stood
But the shore along Your ocean?
Are You fire? Are You fury?
Are You sacred? Are You beautiful?

What do I know, what do I know of Holy?

I guess I thought that I had figured You out
I knew all the stories and I learned to talk about
How You were mighty to save
Those were only empty words on a page
Then I caught a glimpse of who You might be
The slightest hint of You brought me down to my knees

What do I know of Holy?
What do I know of wounds that will heal my shame?
And a God who gave life its name?
What do I know of Holy?
Of the One who the angels praise?
All creation knows Your name
On earth and heaven above
What do I know of this love?

What do I know of Holy?

I think that the simple encouragement in this reflection is that when little around you makes sense, then it is time to learn more about the Father. When all that we are trying seems to be falling a little short, then we need to seek Him out in greater depth. When we are dealing with issues that are overwhelming to us, we need to go to the One who is big enough to handle all things. So it makes great sense that it will help us to know more of Holy.

Let me be clear, I am not saying that the reason that things may be going wrong is because we do not know enough about Him or that we need to be a better believer, not at all. What I am saying is, there is so much to know about our Creator, Lord, and Savior that, when we become lost, the sure solution to being found is to go in search of His holiness.

The whole life of the good Christian is a holy longing. —Augustine

Why do the words of this song resonate with such truth? I believe it is because they give us insight into the reasons why we all struggle. Then, in its searching for an answer, the song gives to us directions for getting there.

Why we might struggle to know of Holy?

I tried to hear from heaven, but I talked the whole time.

How often is God waiting there to share or to inspire us with something, and we just keep talking? And then when we are done, we just hang up and end the conversation. I encourage us to listen to God much more than we do.

I think I made You too small, I never feared You at all, no.

I feel the secret is to be able to fear (be in awe of) His holiness, and to at the same time celebrate the fact that He is the One who "spoke you into motion" for relationship with Him. At the very same time, He is the fire and fury, and He is the sacred. I encourage you to ask Him what that really means to your life. Awesome stuff, this Holiness…

The path to better know of Holy:

If you touched my face… looked into my eyes, could I behold You?

I just want to encourage you that He already does this. And how often do we miss the "presence of Holy" in the caring and compassion of the eyes of a dear friend whom He has sent to be with us? How often do we miss His touch that comes to us in the obvious and the unexpected? We just have to make sure that we are familiar with who He is and then be open to beholding Him.

I have already said that we need to be on an endless journey of seeking Him, and finding out deeper and more intimate truths about Him. The minute that you believe the enemy's lie—"You know enough to get by."—you are toast.

What do I know of holy? No more than you. But I encourage you to join me on a journey to discover all that He has to reveal.

I love this song so much. I continue to play it in my car often, and every time I hear it, I always think that I should write something on it. Then I remember that I already have.

A lot of responses agreed with the point that we probably don't listen enough to God and spend enough time in reflection. We are too busy doing the talking. And a number of people had just heard the song for the first time as well, so the Holy Spirit's timing was right on, as usual.

Holiness can be a delicate balance of awe and intimacy. If we looked into His eyes, how could we not behold Him? The inspiration of the Wind-Fire Moments is to recognize that we can see Him in our everyday lives.

WHOM ARE WE SEEKING?

12/13/2007

There is a saying out there, seen sometimes on bumper stickers or on signs around Christmastime, that says, "Wise men still seek Him." It confuses me a bit; I thought I'd already found Him.

But maybe there's something deeper here. Let's run with the premise that those who are wise are still seeking after Him.

And you will seek Me and find Me, when you search for Me with all of your heart. —Jeremiah 29:13

My question is: whom do you spend your time seeking? Are you seeking the One who came to earth proclaiming that He will heal the brokenhearted and set the captives free?

Or are you caught up in this fast-paced life, one of those who "*loved the approval of men rather than the approval of God*" (John 12:43)? Maybe you are like those whom Paul described in Romans 1:22–25:

Professing to be wise, they became fools and exchanged the glory of the incorruptible God for an image in the form of corruptible man... therefore God gave them over in the lusts of their hearts... for they exchanged a truth for a lie...

Whom do you spend your time seeking? Or perhaps more accurately, *what* do you spend your time seeking?

Is your ability to see the necessary moments of relationship with our Savior clouded by your focus on other matters?

If you are too busy at work, caught up in other activities, seeking the attention of others, or trying to follow and admire those who have been labeled by this world as successful, you have sacrificed your relationship with the incorruptible God to gain recognition from corruptible man. Your vision has become clouded.

We are all guilty of this, are we not? And then when we come to that time of year that focuses on Christmas, the reminder is shouted to us about the One whom we should be seeking to know. I want to encourage your seeking with three examples that we are often reminded of at this time of year:

The Shepherds: They heard the truth from the angels: "Today in the city of David there has been born *for you* a savior" (Luke 2:10). And what was their response? "Let us go straight to Bethlehem then, and see this thing that has happened" (Luke 2:15).

Don't you love that? These simple shepherds are told that a savior has been born for them. And though they may not have been the smartest guys in the region, they made the right choice and went straight to Bethlehem. They did not wait for their shift to end, or until after the bowl games the next day. They did not even choose to pass "Go." *They went straight to Bethlehem.*

Simeon: The Holy Spirit revealed to this elderly man that he would not die until he had seen the Lord Christ (Luke 2:26). And upon seeing the child Jesus, he said, "Now, God, Thou dost let Thy bondservant depart in peace, according to Thy word: For my eyes have seen Thy salvation" (Luke 2:29–30).

This was a man who allowed the Spirit to move in him, and in so doing, stayed committed to his heart and the purpose, which gave him the vision to know that the child before him was the Savior. We need to ask the Spirit to give us that vision to see the moments to embrace God like that.

The Magi: These wise men who specialized in astrology came to Jerusalem, asking, "Where is He who has been born King of the Jews? For we saw his star in the east, and have come to worship Him" (Matthew 2:2).

Here was a group of men who had applied all of their intellectual knowledge to figure out that the star in the sky represented the foretold King. But they then allowed their heart knowledge to drive them to find Him, so that they could worship Him.

The shepherds may not have been seeking at that moment, but they responded to the calling. *Simeon* was on a never-ending quest. *The magi* prepared themselves to be able to recognize the time of His coming, and with eyes able to see, they responded in kind.

So my encouragement to you: know whom you are seeking!

When you hear the truth, act on it right away. Go straight to Bethlehem. Walk with the power of the Holy Spirit in you, that you may be ready to recognize the moments God wants you to embrace. Make time to be still and know that He is God.

You can intellectually gain knowledge of the One that you seek, but also listen to your heart when it says that the time has come to worship.

I don't have any of the comments saved prior to September of 2008. I changed computers and hard drives and just didn't think that some three years down the road, I would have a desire to look back and see what was said.

I know that I love to look at everything that was happening and everyone who was involved around that first Christmas. I don't mean to de-emphasize the significance of the birth of Jesus, but I just like to picture how everyone else who was there handled their encounter with God.

Silent God

09/06/2007

How long will my prayers seem unanswered?
Is there still faith in me to reach the end?
I'm feeling doubt, I'm losing faith
But giving up would cost me everything
So I'll stand in the pain and silence
And I'll speak to the dark night

Though I can't see my story's ending
That doesn't mean the dark night has no end
It's only here that I find faith
And learn to trust the One who writes my days
So I'll stand in the pain and silence
And I'll speak to the dark night

These are words from the beautiful song "I Believe in Love" by Barlow Girl. How many of us have been in this place in at least one point in our spiritual lives? It is a place that seems so dark that we cannot see how we will survive the next years, months, or even days. It is a place where we can just not seem to hear God or to feel the presence of His Spirit. It may be circumstances that the world has thrown at us, or spiritual warfare with the enemy, or it may just be a true season of spiritual dryness.

In a recently released book on Mother Theresa, many were surprised to read that her writings revealed that she lived most of her ministry days in a silent time, where she could not feel God's presence. She found strength through those times in the realization that she was living in the same sort of separation from the Father that Christ must have felt on the cross. Evidently, there is no one immune to this silence.

I have come to believe two things on this subject over the last few years. First, no one knows how someone else feels when going through a dark time. If people say to you, "I know how you must be feeling," the truth is that they really don't. Each time of darkness is a personal matter, and each wound, arrow, or suffering (however you want to describe it) resounds differently within each person. There are just too many factors at work.

And I also believe the only way that you can have true empathy for someone in a dark and hopeless place, is if you yourself have at some time reached that point where everything you can envision ahead has failed, that point where you have to put yourself into God's hands because you cannot see one more step ahead of you.

The second thing that I have come to believe is that, until you have reached that end of your rope, where you finally crawl into God's arms and say "I have nothing left," you may never know the richness of how wonderful your relationship with God can be. It is putting aside all self and experiencing the closeness with God that He has created us to have with Him. It is that experience of being put through the kiln, and then coming out strengthened and shaped into the one He has created you to be. It is being restored back to a state of full Glory.

Mind you, all do not have to reach such a suffering point in their life to find such richness in their relationship with God. But there is something unique that develops from that kind of experience.

How do you handle those times of silence and darkness in your spiritual life? I imagine each of us finds something unique in our own faith during those times that allows us to lock onto the strength to hang on. Here is the chorus to the song that I shared at the beginning. It is taken from words that were found carved into a wall in a concentration camp during the Holocaust, written by a man who had been held prisoner there. These are words that I can lock onto:

I believe in the sun even when it is not shining
I believe in love even when I don't feel it
And I believe in God even when He is silent

I realize the insufficiency of my trying to say anything significant on this topic. But I do want to encourage any of you who are currently going through a silent or dark time: you are not alone. Others are going through struggles as well, no matter how hard they try to pretend that they are not. And knowing that does bring some comfort. The enemy would like you to think that you are the only one who has ever had such a problem. He will tell you that a real Christian wouldn't have your kind of struggle and that you should find shame in your circumstances. They are bald-faced lies! And those lies need to be renounced as soon as you recognize them.

Being authentic, sharing your struggles with those close to you who can be of help, or who can just listen, will do far more good for you than you can imagine. And you will also find that when you share, that there will be others out there who have never been able to put their own similar feelings into words, others who have been waiting to know that they are not alone.

And you are not alone, because God has not left you alone. He never will!

I believe in God even when He is silent!

I believe this to have been the beginning of my crusade for authenticity. This was the time when I first wrote about the "silent" times and the fact that my life was full of struggles.

At first, I was unsure how everyone would respond to it. But it was then that I realized how much people were ready for others to share their struggles, because they too were dealing with some kind of pain. Often, people have said that I have finally put to words what they have been feeling. I hope that it was that and much more. I hope that it also gave them the freedom to be authentic with others when times got tough.

WHY ARE WE SEARCHING?

09/04/2008

Why are you striving these days?
Why are trying to earn grace
Why are you crying, Let me lift up your face
Just don't turn away

Why are you looking for love?
Why are you still searching as if I'm not enough?
To where will you go, child, Tell me where will you run
To where will you run?

And I'll be by your side whenever you fall
In the dead of night whenever you call
And please don't fight these hands that are holding you
My hands are holding you

Look at these hands and my side
They swallowed the grave on that night
When I drank the world's sin
So I could carry you in, and give you life
I want to give you life

—"By Your Side" by Tenth Avenue North

Every time I hear this song on the radio, its questions jump out at me. Why do we keep striving to earn the grace that God has freely given us? Why are we all, believers and non-believers alike, searching to be affirmed by love when God has promised and demonstrated that love in so many ways?

I want this Wind-Fire Moment to be an encouragement to those who are struggling with either or both of these tendencies. First, I want you to know that you are definitely not alone in this struggle. There wouldn't be so many songs about these problems if it were just you. My encouragement is for you to accept the grace He so freely wants to give to you, for you to grab hold and never let go of His love that has been there for you from the beginning of time.

I think God's heart breaks a little every time that He hears someone lament that they are working to earn their way to His love, or that they need to be a better person to be loved fully by Him. They feel unworthy, stuck in a comparison dilemma where they never measure up to what they see from others.

What they forget is that often they only see from others the nicely presented package that those around them put on the Christian stage for their benefit. When you unwrap those packages, you find the same brokenness and struggles that are carried by all of us. The enemy uses this façade of perfection to hold people back, claiming that God's grace is not sufficient to cover our shortcomings, or that God does not have the same kind of love for us as He does for others, or a variety of other lies. But I want to encourage us all to remember that there is not one thing that you can do to make God love you more than He already does.

In preparing to write, the Holy Spirit reminded me of these words from the Matthew West song "Only Grace":

And there's only grace, there's only love
There's only mercy, and believe me, it's enough
Your sins are gone without a trace
And there's nothing left now, there's only grace

The desire to be loved is built into our nature. Love is the core of the relationship with God that we were created for. That is why it is so critical for a child to hear from his or her parents over and over again, "I love you." It is why spouses need to hear constantly from each other those same words.

When we don't sense that we are finding love, we take that old road of "looking for love in all the wrong places, looking for love in too many faces." All along, God is there, wondering why we will not accept His love as enough. It is enough love to build a foundation in our lives, so that we can first love ourselves, and then be open to allow the right kind of love to come in from others.

But we often push God aside, wanting more. We begin to listen to the lie that there is something better out there than the love of our Creator. Sure, in time, we will invite Him in to have a place of honor—as soon as we get things figured out and have our life together enough. Like that will ever happen without Him.

I had most of this Moment already written before I sat down to finish it up. And then on the morning of writing, I asked the Spirit to make sure that I was clear on just what He wanted to get across with this message. He told me not to preach, but to encourage and to speak to the heart. The Spirit told me that the questions in the song are simply from the heart: "Why?" "Why are you all striving?" "Why don't you see that what I offer is enough?" He said, "Say nothing more than that."

As I went to take my shower, I turned on the radio as I always do, and it immediately came on to the Tenth Avenue North song I opened with. He was affirming my message. I heard this line like I was listening for the very first time:

"And please don't fight these hands that are holding you"

I lifted my hands in the air to Him, and the Spirit shouted the words to leave you with:

Please don't fight My hands that are holding you.

I love the intimacy with God that the Tenth Avenue North song talks about. We have a God who loves us so much that He comes to us. And yet we still continue to strive. We still continue to search for something more.

Many people related to this one, as the struggles and brokenness are found everywhere, even in those who put on a good face.

I think that Tenth Avenue North would have to be my honorary Wind-Fire Moment band, in that I have referenced so many songs off of their first CD. Of course, they would have to share the stage with Casting Crowns and Third Day.

WALK WITH GOD

02/04/2008

My friend Jim and I have attended two different men's conferences put on by John Eldredge's ministry group. Both times, the Question-and-Answer sessions contained a number of people eager to ask Eldredge for what he thought God's answer was to a certain situation.

"John, do you think my buddies and I should do our own retreats back home?"

"John, I saw where a number of people were healed at a big revival setting in Brazil. If I want to be a part of a Healing ministry, should I look to spend time at one of these settings?"

And so on.

They always seemed to be looking for him to give them an easy answer as to how God is working, like there is a formula to figuring out God. Jim and I appreciate that John does not believe God always answers situations the same way, since the Bible makes it pretty clear that He does not. To each of these questions, Eldredge would just offer a small suggestion to the thought process they should go through, and then he would end by saying, "Walk with God."

That's it. It is very simple and straight to the point. It is perfect.

What is the answer to my need? Walk with God.

How do I get over my fear or lack of faith? Walk with God.

How do I hear God speak to me through the Holy Spirit? Walk with God.

Is this not the true sense of what our relationship with the Trinity should be all about?

What does it mean to "walk with God," you ask?

Teach me Thy way, O Lord; I will walk in Thy truth:
Unite my heart to fear Thy name.

I will give thanks to Thee, O Lord, my God, with all my heart,
And will glorify Thy name forever.   —Psalm 86:11–12

"Walking with God leads to receiving His intimate counsel, and counseling leads to deep restoration." —John Eldredge

The Lord is my shepherd, I shall not want. He makes me lie down in green pastures; He leads me beside quiet waters. He restores my soul. He guides me in the paths of righteousness...   —Psalm 23:1–3

This is not to say, "You should walk with God daily," like a doctor would tell you, "It is good to exercise daily." The doctor's advice is the type of thing where if you do it, great, you feel better. If you don't, you may miss it at first, but after awhile it doesn't really matter to you.

I am encouraging you to **walk with God!** You should equate this with seeing and breathing. When we wake up in the morning, it takes no conscious effort to see or breathe, it is just a natural process—and it is essential to us. We could choose to close our eyes, but then we would be lost and could not get where we need to go. And if we chose not to breathe...

This should not be a strange concept. You were created by God to have relationship with Him. This is natural and essential. Eldredge likes to say, "I don't choose to walk with God because it is good for me. I do it because I am toast if I don't."

That is the point. We are toast if we don't. This is not, "Make sure that you have a quiet time every morning." This is, "Make sure that you are alive to the Holy Spirit at every moment of your existence." There are times in the day when you are bombarded with conflict or by evil. You should not wait until your morning "quiet time" to deal with them. You should immediately seek His counsel by asking, "God, what is going on here? Give me the eyes to see all that is really attacking me. Give me the wisdom now to know what to do." And He will restore you! He will give you the strength you need.

Lately, I have been needing to ask God to let me see some situations as He does. To see with eyes from a larger-story vantage point. When I do that, the situation that seems so all-encompassing to me looks instead like something that I can manage, and that allows me to find some peace. This has been the only way that I have gotten to sleep some nights. "God, I know that I am exhausted, but I am lying here wide-awake, dealing with this situation. Let me see it with Your eyes, so that I can put it in perspective and then find peace for my spirit. I want to go to sleep!"

I don't think that I could get to that awareness if I was not already attempting to walk with God. As we learn to walk with God and hear His voice, He is able to speak to our wounds, struggles, and crises of faith. Our Heavenly Father truly wants to protect our hearts, and the best way for Him to do that is by allowing Him in on a continuous basis.

And remember, there is no formula for getting this done. There is no required amount of Scripture to read, hours of prayer and meditation to complete, or number of Bible studies to attend. You choose the efforts and amount of time that will keep you connected to Him. But keep the connection going 24/7, not just when it is convenient or because a great need or troubling situation has come into your life.

Just walk it!

I once answered the question, "What do you want your tombstone [epitaph] to say," like this: He loved his wife and family, he walked with God. *It has been a couple of years since then, and I think that I would have to add friends or community right after family, if answering now. But the fact that I did my very best to walk with God daily would still be at the crux of my faith. It acknowledges Him rightly as a living and loving God, and it allows me to get through any and all times.*

Word of God, Speak

08/28/2008

In my preparation for writing this reflection I had been wanting to hear from God. Whether driving around in the car, lying awake in bed or just sitting times of quiet, the mantra was the same. "Word of God, speak, would you pour down like rain. Word of God, speak…" Those words obviously come from the Mercy Me song "Word of God Speak."

I am finding myself at a loss for words, and the funny thing is, it's OK
The last thing that I need is to be heard, But to hear what You would say

Word of God, speak, Would You pour down like rain
Washing my eyes to see Your majesty
To be still and know that You're in this place
Please let me stay and rest in Your holiness
Word of God, speak

I am not sure what I was really looking for. Probably a direct conversation or some sort of "sign" to give my life a little hint of the direction He was going to be leading me in. I think that I was a little confused with how things were coming at me, and I just wanted something clear. Even up to the very morning of finally writing this, I was telling God that I would even be fine with something from Him that simply said, "I love you, Jim." Not that I have any doubts on that, but I could just use the boost.

I want to encourage you to constantly listen for Him and be ready to recognize it when He speaks. And then when He does, be ready to respond. Especially if you are in a time of confusion or doubt, you will find that it is a most beneficial time to be listening for Him to speak.

Just the other day, I had coffee with a very good friend of our family. We were updating each other on what was going on in our lives. This person shared with me some thoughts she had had about a possible new direction in her life. It didn't seem to really strike a chord with me that the thoughts were "inspired." Then she said, "I want to tell you something God said to me recently."

What? We had been talking for probably an hour and a half, and now it comes up that God has recently spoken to her? I kind of half-jokingly said, "Why have you been wasting my time, so far?" With all of the talk that we have had in the past about hearing from God, why would that not be the first topic of conversation? It was a little blunt, I guess.

But once she started talking about this direction that God had spoken to her, her heart came alive with a passion I had seldom seen. This was something my friend had been dreaming about for years, and now there was a chance to begin to explore it. It was so clear to me that God was in this plan, waving His orange airport flashlights and saying, "Come this way." It was fun to see my friend light up with passion and confidence. And it was why I want to encourage all of you to be ready to respond when you hear from Him. And I did ask for forgiveness from my friend for the "wasting my time" comment.

We can also hear from God through His Word. Psalm 119 is filled with verses that are about listening to, trusting, and being taught through His Word:

My soul cleaves to the dust: revive me according to Thy word.
—verse 25

Thy word is very pure, therefore Thy servant loves it.   —verse 40

Thy testimonies are righteous forever; Give me understanding that I may live.   —verse 144

This is where God led me this week: to go to His Word, where He would revive me so that I may live. So I sat down with no more direction than to go to the Bible to hear the Word of God speak. I did what every great Bible scholar does. I said, "God, I have no clue where to go. I am just going to open the Bible and trust that right there I will find what I need." This is not as random as it sounds; all of God's Word has the ability to apply somewhere, but I was amazed to see that God ended up speaking directly to the exact things happening in my life at this moment.

I turned right to Habakkuk 2. Now, I know that no one purposely opens the Bible to Habakkuk 2. It is not in the middle, and believe me, those pages are not tattered and worn in my Bible, though I did find that the verse "But the righteous will live by faith" was already highlighted in yellow. This drew my eyes there, and Habakkuk 2:2–7 spoke great strength and encouragement to me in the situation that I was dealing with. And believe me, the message could only have been brought to me at this time by God answering my calling out to Him.

So this week, call out to Him to speak to you. May you hear it or may you read it. His Word is truth, and it is powerful. Do not let this great source of His wisdom and love go unused in your life. You will find hope and renewed strength from what you read and hear.

Word of God, speak, would you pour down like rain...

I am sad to say that it is closing on three years since I wrote this Moment, and I do not think that I have talked with my friend again about what God had said to her. And it is not because I have not seen her. I am now inspired to contact her and see if she has been able to make that step toward what she felt God had called her to do.

We are so blessed to have the Holy Spirit with us full-time, and we must not let that go to waste.

—SECTION SEVEN—

THE HEART

I was always hesitant to write anything about the heart, because I thought that there was just way too much material to write about to do it justice in one of my weekly writings. So I ended up breaking it out into many topics as the Spirit inspired ideas.

This section, which differs from the Eyes of the Heart section, deals a lot with caring for your heart and making sure that you have it in action, working properly. You will find the encouragement to let God hold your heart so that you can make it through the challenging times and the encouragement to constantly ask others how their heart is doing.

We are all in constant need of tuning up and recharging our hearts, and I hope that you will find that these reflections will encourage you in such a way.

A Crushed Heart

04/08/2010

The other day, I was sitting in a Starbucks, finishing up a Wind-Fire Moment. At a table just to the right of me, a man was waiting for someone. After a while, a young woman came up to him with a smile. I didn't quite catch the greeting between the two, but I caught what came next.

The gal was his daughter, and he was the dad who no longer lived at home. She was meeting him there to bring him what looked like a cell-phone charger for the car. She had brought the wrong item. And he proceeded to let her have it. He made it clear that he had driven a long way that morning and that he had been waiting for a while. He attacked her for being lazy and just sitting around, and for not having a job. He blamed her for not thinking and for not respecting him. (I wanted to scream some interference.) He took time to attack the mother (his ex) for her handling of the girl and her brother. She sat silently and took it. I can only assume that her heart was crushed. I know mine was.

I must say, in fairness, that the dad recovered well. By the end, he was showing her how to fill out a deposit slip for the check he was writing her as an allowance of some sort. He showed to how to follow that account online on her phone. He told her it was her money to spend how she wished, and he gave her some positive thoughts. (Hey, I was sitting really close.) He had brought a couple of little decorative storage boxes for her, and she was excited to show him something new. Her heart seemed to rebound. I know mine did.

It was tough to witness, but it made me think about how many times our hearts are beaten down or crushed, especially when our hearts enter into a situation with positive hopes, as it seemed to be in the case of this girl. It made me wonder about the times that our hearts are not given that opportunity to recover so quickly. What wounds would we carry with us after such an event? As it seems to be my calling to encourage the hearts of others to be alive, I pondered these things deeply.

We are fortunate that we will never come to our Heavenly Father with a heart of joy and have it beaten down by Him. Granted, our hearts' desires are not always fulfilled when we go to Him, but He will never deliver blows that will leave our hearts wounded. That, unfortunately, is what we to do to each other. His love for us is so great that it is always a place of both adventure and sanctuary.

As I often do, I encourage you this week to watch over the heart, not only to watch over your own but to be an ambassador of the heart in regards to others.

Guard from being the one to wound. As I watched that father talk to his daughter, I wanted to grab him and say, "Don't take out your bad day on her." For that is what it seemed was happening. How often do we do that to someone else? We find ourselves struggling with our personal situations or feeling guilty over something we have done, and we end up taking it out on someone else. The result is, we tear down the heart of that person. As an ambassador, I encourage you to stay on the alert to prevent this from occurring.

Seek God for sanctuary. The truth is, even while you may be on sentry duty, it is rare that your heart will escape getting wounded at times. It may come from someone who consciously says or does something that leaves a scar or from one who has no idea what they have done. In either case, we must seek healing as soon as we can. Long-lingering wounds will only fester into something worse. This is where God's sanctuary will provide a way for us to recover. I am afraid that the girl in the scene that I witnessed would not have the inclination to address her wounds right away; it is a lesson that most people have not learned. I would just hate to see her have to deal with uncared-for scars later in life.

Seek God for adventure. Do you want to keep your heart in good condition? Then you need to take it out for a spin every once in a while, have a little adventure. This can be simply defined as finding that which makes your heart come alive and doing it. It may be what you do for your vocation, hobby, ministry, or recreation. It is taking the gifts that God has given you and putting them into action so that your true calling begins to reflect His glory brightly. The heart is alive and strong when it is active and full of this joy.

Let's do this together. Let's work to keep hearts alive and well. Be on alert for those hearts that have taken a beating, and do what you can to comfort them and begin a healing process. And always, be on guard for you own heart. It is the only one you've got.

This is another one of those personal favorites that when I look at it, my heart kind of leaps. I have a little sense of, "I am glad I wrote that." I am a self-proclaimed encourager of the heart, and this was a story that just needed to be shared.

I got a mixture of responses here. A teacher sees this type of behavior from parents who crush the spirit of their kids and then wonder why they turn out the way they do. Another person would focus all week on the quote, "be an ambassador of the heart in regards to others."

HOLD MY HEART

10/22/2009

One night while I was at home, my daughter Katie asked me if I had time to watch a YouTube video. It turned out to be a recording of two members of the band Tenth Avenue North talking about and then singing the song "Hold My Heart." (A good friend of mine says that I most often write about one of my kids or a song, and so there you have both of those mentioned in paragraph one.)

The writer of the song said that growing up as a Christian, he felt he always had to have an answer for every question. He grew up under the delusion that Christianity was about a bunch of right answers, not realizing that at the heart of Christianity is an encounter with a person.

So many questions without answers
Your promises remain
So I think I will take my chances
To hear You call my name
Hear You call my name...

I referenced the words to this song over a year ago, but God has just been pounding it back into my heart to use again. At one point on a three-day driving journey a few weeks ago, I played this song six times in a row. It was a lot of driving.

One tear in the pouring rain
One voice in the sea of pain
Could the maker of the stars
Hear the sound of my breaking heart

Recently, I got a chance to share again in front of some Christian business-people at a breakfast gathering. As before, I spoke of my walking with God through the jungle that seems to just go on and on. I finished by saying that there was no great Job-like ending yet to this story, and that God had yet to swoop in and make everything great. Yet I concluded, as I always do, by saying that God has never promised me that I will not have struggles or that businesses will always be sound and I will be financially secure, but He does promise that He will love me and that He will always be with me.

Talking with people afterwards, it was made clear to me again how many others are going through their own struggle-filled journeys. They seemed to find comfort knowing they are not the only ones.

One life, that's all I am
Right now I can barely stand
If You are who You say You are
Would You come close and hold my heart

Would You Hold my Heart... Hold my heart

So my encouragement is to everyone who is struggling because you don't have the answers to all the questions, and it worries you that you don't. I know that some of these questions are impacting our lives greatly and causing us to call out to God for some explanation. I know that these tough questions exist:

Why am I (or someone close to me) ill and not being healed?

How do I deal with the death of a loved one?

Why has my marriage struggled or failed?

Why can't I get out of this financial struggle?

Why, when I am surrounded by so many people, do I often feel alone?

Is this what God really wants for my life?

Why does it seem that some of my prayers are not answered?

If you took a moment and went through these questions again, but this time followed each one with *So, God, would You hold my heart?* could you see the impact?

During the midst of trials, I cannot think of a more important request that I could make to Him than to hold my heart. It fills me with great passion to say (sing) that line. As I lie in bed at night, looking to settle my body and spirit down so I may find some rest in peaceful sleep, I find great comfort in repeating, "Will You hold my heart?" With each utterance, the depth of my sincerity grows, as does the depth of the truth of His love for me.

The message is simple: free yourselves from the burden of needing an answer to everything. Just as it is said in the Steven Curtis Chapman song, "God is God, and I am man. So I'll never understand it all... Only God is God." If you replace your frustration of not knowing the answers with the freedom of not having to know, you will find great relief.

God, will You hold my heart?

Will You hold my heart?

Hold my heart...

I feel much better! You should give it a try.

The encouragement to lie in bed at night and ask God to hold your heart is such a good reminder to all of us. I for one can say that I have lost the practice of it.

I had a number of people just respond to me with "Thank you, I needed that" or just "Thank you." A good friend was teaching a study to a group of women on "Lies Women Believe" that she said was truly parallel to this message.

How Is Your Heart?

09/24/2009

It is time for me to ask that essential question to each and every one of you: *How is your heart?*

If, when thinking about how you might answer this question, you didn't pause and give a long sigh, then you probably didn't get the depth of what I was asking you. This is not a surface-level question that can be answered with *Fine, OK,* or *Good*. This is a question that is intended for diving and swimming in deep waters, and for some of you, those waters might be uncharted.

How is your emotional command center? It is that area of your heart that manages your relationship with God, with family, and with friends. It also has to deal with the daily challenges that are thrown at you in work and personal life, not to mention your dreams and desires.

Let me rephrase it one more time. How are you doing in stepping out from all the "little story" issues that bog down your life and numb your heart? Are you stepping up and into living, front and center, on the stage of God's bigger story, where things matter most?

Sigh! OK, so now you get it.

So, how is your heart? Would you even be able to tell me? Have you taken the time lately to take a visit to that part of you or even to think about it? Are you doing anything to make sure that this area in your life is healthy?

So let my encouragement come to you in the way of a reminder. It is a reminder to recognize the importance of not only paying close attention to your own heart, but to the condition of the hearts of others. I know we are all aware of these things, but sometimes we just need to have our consciousness shaken up a little.

Reminder 1: You need to protect and care for your heart.

Do not let the enemy come and steal your heart. That is his plan, and if he cannot fully take it away, he will work to leave it wounded. And know that the enemy is capable of wounding in such a way that you may find it a long process to heal. For some, the healing can take a lifetime. This can often happen when you leave your heart unattended. You need to condition your heart to be strong, and you need to connect to God at the deepest depths.

Reminder 2: When your heart is strong, you will be able to support the hearts of others.

Part of the call of community is to watch over one anothers' hearts. Just watch how people light up when you ask about the areas in their lives that they are passionate about. When you make the decision to pursue with sincerity their hearts, below the surface-level discussions, you will witness new strength come pumping into their spirits. Reaching out to encourage the heart of someone else can also be a part of your wound-healing process.

Reminder 3: Know what to take to others and what needs to go to God.

John Eldredge, in his *Waking the Dead* writes, "Be careful about what you are looking for from Community. For if you bring your every need to it, it will collapse. Community is no substitute for God." To translate for all of you who are tech-savvy, "some files are a little too large to download to the human hard-drive." Community is there for encouragement and support, but for major repairs, you need to direct your calls to the factory, your Creator, who is the Great Healer and Counselor, and He is "able" and "standing by," waiting for your call.

I want to encourage you to take time to get together with others to talk about the heart. That will be a good way for you to know that you are watching out for your own. You can simply ask someone in an e-mail, "How is your heart?" Or better yet, go and grab a coffee or something that will give you a time and place for a little discussion.

And I will say again that if someone will authentically begin to answer this question for you, it will be preceded by a deep breath or a large sigh. The heart has its ups and downs, and there should never be a lack of something to talk about.

By the way, how is your heart? Take some time. You should know.

This message touched the hearts of so many, who admitted to having a neglected heart. I even got a very honest response from someone in high school who shared with me that things were not going that well. And many said it helped them to remember the importance of guarding the heart.

With All of Your Heart

02/18/2010

Can you think of anything that you do with all of your heart, something that you are so passionate about that you put it on priority above all else?

Look at a rabid sports fan—to be more specific, a college or pro football fan. When their favorite team plays a game, they will make sure that they have the day off from work; they will skip church and blow off any family planning for the day. They must be at the game or at the least watching the game somewhere, in their team jersey. Their mood is thoroughly dictated by the outcome of the game. And then during the week, they may be studying the stats for a fantasy football league or watching all the wire-reports to stay up on the latest league gossip. That is giving a lot of your heart.

What else can you give your whole heart to, where you are willing to sacrifice all else for the cause? How about the student-athlete who sacrifices school and social life for giving their whole heart to their sport? There, of course, is the person dedicated to a job, the workaholic. They give their whole heart to their career, sacrificing family and other things. Others give their heart to a hobby, a television series, or a social life. The fact is, there are things to which we will give our whole heart out of passion to the cause.

*You will seek Me and find Me, when you search for Me **with all of your heart**... and I will be found by you... and I will restore [what you have lost]...*   —Jeremiah 29:13–14

I want that! We all know these verses. They are quoted all the time and used in worship songs. But I took an extra hard look at it lately because I so wanted to claim His promise. And in looking, my question to myself was, "What does it look like to search for Him with *all of my heart*?"

I know that I pray to Him very earnestly when I am in need. But is that giving Him all of my heart? Or does that just give Him my scared and worried heart at that moment in time?

I encourage you to seek out what it means to search for Him with all of your heart. What would it mean to you?

Would your attitude for the week be dictated by whether or not you had found Him that week?

If I put aside my constant search for God, I find myself totally out of sorts. I am less able to handle stress, and I know that I am less open to some of the songs on the radio to touch my spirit. And why will I have put off my search for Him? It is probably because I will have given greater priority to other matters, like too much time with my newspaper in the morning or the TV at night. Or it will be that during the day I would rather fill my ears with listening to people talk on the radio instead of taking that same time to find some quiet to hear from Him.

Would you make sure that you had put off other plans so that you could be sure to have some time with Him?

Would you skip watching your team play an early game on TV so you could go to worship God in community? We will skip church for the game, but will we reverse that? Will you make it a priority to get some time in with Him (anywhere or anytime), like you might do with your exercise routine or your time on Facebook? Ouch! I know that was a shot at a few people there.

I have to be clear with everyone: I am just as bad as anyone else at this. I can quote lines from movies and remember which actor or actress was in movies I have never seen, but I cannot quote as many Scriptures or always keep straight the names of the 12 disciples. I guess that I would probably be in the same boat as my dad, who is fond of saying something to effect that, "If the disciples would have had numbers on their backs, I could probably remember them."

Your walk can certainly be strong without knowing a ton of Scripture or reciting the books of the Bible, but the message here is that the knowledge you pick up makes a point about where you heart is at. If we would all just look at

His promise to us, we should all wonder why we are not making stronger efforts to search after Him with all of our hearts.

And I will be found by you... and I will restore [what you have lost]...

Again I will say, *I want that!* The Bible actually says, "...and I will restore your fortunes." I replaced "fortune" with "what you have lost" because I figured that we may all have different kind of fortunes that have been lost. Some are financial, some spiritual, and some personal like a marriage or friendships. The point is that His promise is to restore. The point is that you will find Him. And it is not like that search is very hard, because He is always there for you.

It just comes down to you deciding to do the seeking with all of your heart.

Of course, since I wrote this particular Moment, including its shot at Facebook users, I have finally joined Facebook myself. I even had to write a Wind-Fire Moment about that. Of course, I used the excuse that I needed to do it to help market the book.

People responded honestly that they could not think of anything they do with their whole heart. One person wrote that this was a home run with three men on base, and another said I hit the nail hard with this one.

Someone said this was all very true and that "life" gets in the way of what should be the priority of our life. This person continued, saying that we are drawn away from our Lord by the very subtle lies of the evil one.

—SECTION EIGHT—

THE FANTASTIC FOUR

Obviously, I think that all of the reflections in this book are fantastic, but I really could not figure out which category to put these very special writings in. So in an attempt to be creative and fun, and because I enjoyed watching the cartoon when I was young, I have named this section "The Fantastic Four."

I am not sure that I can think of more diverse topics than these four; they all touch the heart in very different places. From the story of a man who, through his preaching, is rescuing young women enslaved in prostitution, to finding the joy of our faith in a childhood game, they cover a lot of area.

Though each differs from the others, I was affirmed in each one of them by the responses I received upon sending them out to readers. My prayer is that you will find that the Spirit will speak to you through them as well.

PROMISE AND THE 3 D'S

04/09/2009

There is something in every one of you that waits and listens for the sound of the genuine in yourself. It is the only true guide you will ever have. And if you cannot hear it, you will all of your life spend your days at the ends of strings that someone else pulls.

—Howard Thurman

It's funny how the Spirit chooses to deliver me my inspiration for a topic. Sometimes I have them stacked up and ready to go. At other times, like with this one, it was Tuesday (which means only two days left until my self-imposed Thursday deadline), and I did not have a clue.

I had always wanted to use the quote that I end this week with, but I just did not have an idea to build it on. Then I chose (or was led) to go to a breakfast meeting with a group of guys. Three of the four of the men at this breakfast, I had never met before, and if you know me, you know that is something I usually avoid. I was outside my normal comfort zone. But, hey, I am trying to grow here.

So at the breakfast, I heard a story of a Nigerian pastor named Promise (one of the best names ever) in the Belgium city of Antwerp. His church was visited by some Nigerian women, and afterwards he asked them if he could visit them. They said that he would not want to visit, because they lived in the red-light district.

These women had been caught up in the trafficking of young girls, taken from their country with the promise of European glamour and riches, or just kidnapped, and all were forced into prostitution. The story is involved, but the end of it is that, since those first visits to his church, he has rescued 700 girls and women from the streets and out of prostitution.

When these brainwashed and threatened girls finally grab their stuff with the courage to get ready to leave, the madams ask them where they are going. "I am going with Promise," is the answer. YES! And now, even the madams are starting to come to the church.

When Pastor Promise is dealing with the women, he never calls them prostitutes, only women who have been thrust into the life of prostitution. After they are rescued, they begin a program that follows this progression:

DISCOVER who you are,

DEVELOP who you are,
And then,

DEPLOY to where and what God wants you to be.

Awesome! I often talk about stepping up to the glory that God has created for us to live in, but I have never really had a way to give direction to that. I have approached each of these three "D's" over that time, but I've never put them together like this.

So let me encourage you not only to see God for who He is and celebrate the victories, but to try these steps to help you on your way to living fully for Him, fully alive, and to dwell in the abundant richness of that relationship with Him.

Discover who you are: I can totally relate to this. My very first Wind-Fire Moment talked about when I was challenged to ask God, "Who am I to You, God?" It was a time when I had to push aside the condemning thoughts of the enemy so that I could hear my God/Creator/Intimate Friend give me a glimpse into the glory for which I was made. For me, I heard from Him that very afternoon as I sat on that hillside in Colorado.

For others, I know that discovery can be a much longer process. It is a journey in itself to listen to the Spirit and to hear feedback and affirmation from those who are close to you. This is a good example of the importance of having a close-knit group of people around you. Call them Life Groups, Home Fellowships, Band of Brothers, or just dear friends—just have them in your life. It can be two to three people or it can be six to eight, or whatever size will actually deliver the ability to go very deep, where you have total trust in them to know that they are faithful to be a part of your journey.

Develop who you are: Does this process ever really stop? As a matter of fact, I am not sure any of these processes ever stop. For me, I know that it is an ongoing process of developing ways that I can be His "wind." How will I encourage, move, challenge, disrupt, and bring a cooling presence to others? Will it be through writing something every week or by speaking at a Christian Businesspersons' Breakfast, as I recently did?

Will it be through my monthly Third Thursday Bistro, which is filled with great stories from the people who have come? Or maybe it will just be accomplished by whatever I am doing that is a reflection of His glory. And since our God is infinite in His wonder and glory, I can be assured that my reflection of that glory will never stop being and developing.

Deploy who you are: Now here is where it gets fun—really, it does! I can attest to the joy that comes when you find yourself living in your element, if you will. When you are in the midst of developing, and you reach that *Aha!* moment, you realize, "Yes, this is real. This is what God meant for me."

It will not always be an easy process to sustain or even to begin. Even though we have done some discovering and developing, we still will have to break through much of our past that wants to cling to us. We will have to thwart the enemy's constant attempts to derail us. As we become stronger in our journey, he only becomes angrier. The enemy will continue to taunt you that this is all false or that your past is too scarred for you to achieve what you are setting out to do.

I think of those Nigerian women, who had spent a great deal of time being told that the life they were in was all that they were good for. They were convinced that those around them were the only ones that they could trust. They were lied to that they were no longer lovable to anyone else. I mean, how do you overcome that?

Through God's Promise.

My hope in encouraging you to look at discovering, developing, and deploying is that you may come fully alive. It is the secret to finding the strength to make it on your journey, as well as the true richness in living out your glory.

Don't ask yourself what the world needs. Ask yourself what makes you come alive, and go do that, because what the world needs is those who have come alive.
—Howard Thurman

Out of that group of men that I had to talk myself into going to breakfast with that morning, I have been meeting with two every week for over the last two years.

One person wrote and thanked me for being obedient and open to God's wisdom, and for applying it to our growth. She said she was so proud. Thanks, Mom.

THE OTHER SIDE OF WOMEN'S GLORY

10/30/2008

Recently, I sent an email out to about a dozen women, from age 15 to 50-ish in range. What I asked them was this:

"I would like you to tell me two or three women (from real life or literature/ film) that you personally regard as the most courageous/heroic figures. Then tell me the characteristics about them that put them on the top of the list."

You see, women are often portrayed in story or film as the enabler, the companion, or the object of rescue. Their characteristics are highlighted by how soft, tender, caring, and (most often) how pretty they are. All of which is very good and inspiring, but I wanted to know what really inspired the hearts of women in a more passionate, adventurous, and dramatic way. What was it that invoked in them a passion to admire these other women? I wanted to be able to write a Wind-Fire Moment that inspires and encourages people to see women for the other elements of glory that God created them with.

The responses that I got were amazing. In a few instances, the response was a full page. Not only did they talk about these other women but also how it was just inspiring to be able talk about the topic. I need to rely on the Holy Spirit to help me paint the picture of this message, so that it can be done justice. In the end, I think that it will be best to let the words of others carry most of the message.

I must share one woman's personal response to this topic, because it reached right to the heart of what I was trying to draw out:

"...in this world, people don't see, really SEE who women are, or can be if they are free to be... We (some of us anyway, if we are brave enough to be ourselves) are completely compassionate, feeling, empathizing, truth-telling, life-giving warriors. We get shut down, shut out, and redefined by people around us, media, and our

culture. And some of us give in and just be what people expect. But if you look inside, under a couple of protective layers... you'll see much more."

Can you not just see a heart so passionate, fighting to be fully alive right there? It is so awesomely said, and I think, speaks for many. Hers is a heart that believes fully in this other side of God's glory that is never drawn out of a woman, or worse yet, often covered up.

And it is this other side that was seen in the courageous women that were at the heart of the responses to me: with boldness to "break a mold," having a "zeal for life," living out their faith, and for "embracing all that you are and believing in yourself."

I got a full range of courageous/heroic women cited in the responses. And I want to list as many as I can here, with the inspirational qualities that were mentioned.

I, of course, enjoyed the references inspired by Literature and Film, in that someone was inspired at one point to write these types of characters from qualities they believed come from a woman:

Elizabeth Bennett from *Pride & Prejudice*: "She was not the norm, and I love how she is her own person and shares her ideas and opinions regardless of the context she lives in."

Rose from *Titanic*: "That end scene where it pans over the pictures of her life—that she was able to make the tough decision to start from nothing, leaving everything she knew, to start a new life away from all the expectations."

Arwen from *The Fellowship of the Ring*: She is tender to an injured Frodo, and then carries him on horseback, being chased by the evil black riders, and eventually turns to face them, proclaiming, "If you want him, come and claim him!" Then through a magical incantation (prayer, if you will), she raises up the water of the river (Red Sea-like) to defeat the evil followers.

There were cultural and Biblical women who inspired as well:

Condoleezza Rice: "for being a powerful figure in foreign policy... a man's world."

Janet Kataha Museveni, First Lady of Uganda: "with her husband, helping to confront the AIDS crisis in her country head-on, and breaking barriers to educate their citizens."

Esther: "for her boldness and daringness." Another said for "standing up to incredible pressure in a time when women had NO clout. She changed the course of history with her complete confidence and faith in what was right and what she believed to be true."

Martha: For her pure honor and esteem of Christ.

And finally, and most intimately, there were women whom the women actually lived with. These were everyday people who have fought through illness, been faithful mentors to others, and have lived exemplary lives of faith. I got a few teachers, coaches, grandmothers, friends, and a sister. I got daughters being inspired by mothers, and mothers being inspired by their daughters:

Teachers: "so filled with the Holy Spirit and so excited about God. It always makes me hungry to live for God when I'm with her." And another: "She is an example to her children and the children she teaches... she never puts up a front. She knows who she is—she's God's, and she's confident in that."

A friend: "She simply studied her Bible, had faith that God was who He said He was and that He would and could do all that He said He would. She had faith that God was, is, and will be in control of all things for all time."

A mother and sister: "who both have courage, are strong and independent and totally interesting (in comparison to the norm)."

A daughter: This one produced a whole, heartfelt page, and I will try and encapsulate the thoughts of a mother who describes her daughter as one of her biggest heroes:

"Having a mind of her own, but showing much compassion and mercy at the same time... A natural, born leader, who has had to deal with a life-changing medical issue, never complaining or asking "why me," when we wondered "why her"... Adventured out and made our faith her own... Followed her lifelong passion for her job... Went through a tough personal issue that came with some 'cultural church' shame, but she led everyone through it with a courageous spirit and rock-solid faith..." And finally this mom says that during the birth of a child that brought some complications, *"I would look deep into her eyes and see that she knew everything was going to be good... not easy... but, in the end, good... no matter what the outcome."*

Wow. I think she is now one my heroes, too.

There you have it. If those stories and descriptions do not inspire you to see this wonderful side of God's glory in the heart of women, then I think you might be beyond hope. And I still left out a lot of stories of the battles with major illness, single moms, prayer-warrior grandmothers, and much, much more. By all means very courageous and heroic, but I am already at my longest WFM ever.

Final note: calling this the "other side" of women's glory certainly means that there are two sides, with one being no more important than the other. And I am not out to diminish one by celebrating the other. I just feel that this side needs to be called out more, and the passion in the voices I heard confirms that to me.

So I encourage all women (and girls) to set free that courageous and heroic spirit that God has created you with. Pull away those protective layers and let His full glory shine.

I loved writing this one. I think because it was both a topic that isn't written about enough and it was probably surprising to some that I (being a guy) would write it. But I know that it must have been a topic that stirred the heart, because the woman who helped edit the book dropped in two of her own opinions in the editing notes next to the original comments.

One woman wrote and said that this had put language to some of the issues that she had been pondering for a while. And a good friend shared this with a woman who is an author who writes about strong women, and she wrote, "Loved this!! Cried over it! Wow. Someone that wants to hear the hearts of women. There are so many untold stories of heroism. I pray He gives me a few of them."

Another woman—the one who wrote, "in this world, people don't see, really SEE who women are, or can be if they are free to be..."—went on to write a wonderful half-page more telling me about wonderful women in her life. She said she sent this on to her daughter.

Then I had a father who said he was sending it on to his three girls. A little while later, he forwarded me a response from one of them who said it was really cool, and then went on to thank him for being there for them, saying that she was lucky that God gave her such a dad. How cool is that!

THE VOICE TELLS A STORY

11/11/2010

Every so often, I hear back from people about a Wind-Fire Moment that has made them tear up a little, like someone who read about my dog passing away who had just lost their own dog. Or maybe it was the memory of a family moment that stirred up a shared emotional impact. And when I wrote about my daughter's last soccer match, I had people reply that they were typing their response back to me while looking through the tears in their eyes.

Well, today I am the one having to focus on my typing through tears.

Many of you may be puzzled when I tell you the reason for my tears, though for some of you, it will fully make sense. You see, I just spent the morning reading articles on the passing of Dave Niehaus, the only radio voice there had ever been for the Seattle Mariners.

It is 6:50 on Thursday morning, and I have decided to start a whole new Wind-Fire Moment, instead of finishing the one that I had just about ready to go. I didn't get home from my new job until 11:20 last night, and I have to leave for work again today by probably 8:40, so this is ambitious, to say the least, to think I can write it.

But it is something that must be done. You see, to someone who attempts to find something each week that will encourage the hearts of others, I long to find words that will be alive to you and that will reach out to your heart. I have said I want to write with the spiritual heart of Oswald Chambers, but to have you see it as if viewing a Norman Rockwell painting. I always want there to be the emotion of something authentic from my heart in it. I want to always tell a story. That is why I must write this today.

I want to encourage us all to live lives that tell stories that will positively impact the lives of others. I want to encourage us all to be authentic in ways that will allow people to say, "I can see just who that person is." Just like Dave Niehaus could describe a spring day in Arizona during a boring exhibition game, and you could feel the warmth of the sun and smell the freshly cut grass of that meticulously manicured outfield.

I want to encourage all of us to live with a smile on our face and eyes that have that little sparkle, because we are passionate about our walk with God and we are passionate about living out a glory that was carved out specifically for us. Just the way Niehaus was always excited about Opening Day of the season at Safeco Field.

I write this today because the game of baseball is one my great passions. And whether or not all the girls in my family share the same passion for the Seattle Mariners that my son and I (and my dad and mom) do, we have many emotional bonds together with them. And Dave Niehaus was the orator of many of those memories.

I only need to recall the greatest emotional moment in my sports-fan life, the greatest moment in the history of the Seattle Mariners, and the greatest call in the career of Dave Niehaus, to bring it all together. It was that Sunday afternoon in October of 1995 (just the mention of the year 1995 brings all Mariners fans to full emotional attention), at the culmination of a most amazing five-game series with New York Yankees, when Edgar Martinez's double down the left field line scored Joey Cora from third to tie the game, and brought Ken Griffey, Jr. all the way from first base to slide into home plate and win both the game and the divisional series. I was at the game with my wife, and we hurried to the car as soon as the game was over. I had just seen the play happen right in front of me, but I had to get to the car to hear the post-game replay of Niehaus making the call:

"Here comes Junior rounding third... they're going to wave him home, the throw from the outfield is going to be late... and the Mariners are going to play for the American League Pennant... MY, OH MY!"

It has been 15 years, and I may have missed a few words there, but I just pulled that right from the heart, as I sit here and type. You see, my son, Michael, was just six years old that October in '95, and we had gone to the playoff game just the day before, when Edgar had hit the most famous of all *Get out the mustard and rye bread, Grandma, it's Grand Salami time* home runs to help win Game Four.

Then, for that Christmas, Michael got the video of the 1995 Mariners season, and there is not one of us in this house that will not account for the endless number of times that he played that video. I am sure that throughout all of those times, I never missed shedding a tear when the replay of the Edgar double to score Junior was played. Niehaus recapped that amazing season, building to that one moment.

I took all of my kids to Mariners games when they were three or four—as soon as my wife deemed them old enough for me to be allowed to take them into Seattle by myself to a game. And there was not one of them who would not sit through a whole game with me, even at that young age. Maybe it was because Stephanie would be waiting for a late-inning ice cream cone (and avoiding the Mariner Moose, wherever he was), or Katie waiting for the cotton candy person to come around. And while both girls will tell you that they like watching football best, they know that they were raised on baseball, and raised with Dave Niehaus' voice.

One of the Seattle sportswriters started his column today by saying, "Pardon me, but I must write these words while wiping away my wife's tears." She apparently had never met the Voice of the Mariners, though her husband had many times, but to her Niehaus was "like Disneyland. It's safe, and it's happy because it always the same..."

And now Mariners baseball will never be the same. I asked my wife when I saw her this morning, "Did you hear that Dave Niehaus passed away?" I practiced that line a few times before saying it out loud, because I did not want to start crying while getting it out. "Oh yes, we watched it all last night." Even to the least of the baseball lovers in this house, it was something to be aware of. A woman came back from a break at work last night and told me the news. She didn't know if I liked baseball, but it was news she had to share.

So I write all of this to say, live your life telling a story! Tell a story that will encourage the hearts of others! Whether you do it with actions or words, do it so people's lives are better because of it. Let an authentic heart shine out to others so that they will feel more alive because of it. Just the way that Dave Niehaus shared the game of baseball and life to all of us in Seattle.

It is now 8:05 a.m., and I have to shower for work. But I got to empty my heart out onto this page, and I feel much better for having done so.

I know that not everyone is a baseball fan, and so you may not have quite the appreciation for this story that many did. But we all have a voice, and there is a grand story to both live and tell.

I got so many responses to this. Someone said how amazing it would be if we could all make that kind of contribution in life. One person had to stop after the second paragraph because they had tears in their eyes. (Of course that was a Seattle Mariners fan.) Another friend wrote and asked, "Why did you have to go there?" This friend was at an eye appointment and was glad for the eye dilation because it gave an excuse for the tears.

And many appreciated the tribute and reminisced about some of their favorite baseball memories and how Dave Niehaus had taught them to love the game.

EVERYBODY FREE

11/01/2007

One day my daughter Katie and I were playing some of our classic Christian CDs in the car, when we came across this gem by Michael W. Smith, found on his *This is Your Time* CD. It is a song that moves my heart each time I hear it. It compares the childhood game Hide and Seek to our spiritual search. Please read the words carefully. They are so real to our hearts' quest.

The longing in my heart has stirred a faded memory
Of my young heart beating fast behind the willow tree
I was counting out loud, and I only peeked a time or two
And the only purpose in my life was finding you
Singing, "Ollie, Ollie, everybody free"
Now was I chasing you or were you chasing me?

We all grow up and put away our childhood games
But deep inside I wonder if we really change
Cause I'm still seeking, though I've learned to hide so well
And I can still remember how it felt
Singing, "Ollie, Ollie, everybody free
Will I ever find someone pursuing me?

Chorus
Then You caught me by surprise
I found my tears are in Your eyes
I hear my heart inside of You
At last I've found somebody who
Can free my soul
And love me too

I can't believe we hide so long and run so well
When all the while we're aching to be caught and held
But it's only in surrender that our freedom comes
And so I run abandoned to Your waiting arms
Singing, "Ollie, Ollie, everybody free"
I belong to you and you belong to me

—"Everybody Free" by Michael W. Smith

This song speaks to such basic longings of our souls. "Will I ever find someone pursuing me?" As little children, we long for our parents to love and pursue us. As we grow older, we want the other kids to like us and invite us into their group, we want to be chosen for teams, to be wanted by colleges, hired by employers. And of course, what heart does not long to be pursued by another? Throughout *our whole spiritual journey*, we spend our time seeking to find an answer; all the while, the Answer is pursuing us. From nearly the beginning, we have been doing this: *And the Lord God called to the man, and said to him, "Where are you?"* —Genesis 3:9

But still we "hide so long and run so well, all the time aching to be caught and held." Does that sound familiar to anyone? We are often so unsure of ourselves that we think it is better to hide our true selves away, so that we do not risk being rejected. If that doesn't work, we just stay so busy that we don't allow anyone to catch us and find out who we really are. Inside, though, what we really want and need is for God to catch us and hold us to tell us that we are OK, that we have a purpose. Then, with that confidence, we can go in strength and risk with others. We were made for community, and that is where we need to end up being. The purpose of the game Hide and Seek, after all, is to bring everyone back into community, is it not?

"I found my tears are in Your eyes... I hear my heart inside of You." Can this not be said only of the very One who created us? The very One who truly understands the pain that we have gone through? And it was His heart which was used as the very pattern to create our own. He has made us all in His image. That may be why it is often said, "I am finally home," by those who come to know the Savior after so many years of searching.

"It is only in surrender that our freedom comes." Surrender your need to be in control. Surrender your desire to hold on so tightly to things that will not last. Surrender your life of running from the truth and from the Larger Story that God is calling you into. Then you will find the freedom to celebrate your glory as God intended for you to.

"At last I've found somebody who can free my soul and love me too!" How cool is that! Is that not the true power and message of the gospel? In Jesus' first public speaking, in a synagogue in Nazareth, he quoted from Isaiah 61:1 to describe the purpose of His ministry: *"He has sent me to heal the broken-hearted and to bring freedom to the captives."* He will forgive our imperfections, and thus free us from the condemnation that comes from being spiritually captive to the evil one. Jesus promises that He will love us unconditionally and heal our broken hearts. If more Christians would share the simplicity of *that* gospel to the unsaved, wouldn't more of them come running to Jesus?

My encouragement to you is, wherever you find yourself on this path, that you take action. *Do not wait any longer.* If you are hiding, come on out. If you are running, it is time to slow down. If you are still seeking, stop looking and turn around. If you are broken-hearted, let Him heal you. If you are allowing sin to hold you captive in a life of condemnation, He has opened the gates, cut the chains, and given you your release.

The Author of all things is pursuing you to tell you that he loves you, that you have what it takes, and that He wants to bring restoration to the relationship that He desires the two of you to have.

Now the Lord is the Spirit; and where the Spirit of the Lord is, there is freedom. —2 Corinthians 3:17

Hey everyone! Ollie, Ollie, everybody free!

I had always wanted to tell a lot of people about this song and the message inside it. So I guess the Wind-Fire Moment gave me that chance. I don't have the comments saved from that time (over three years ago), but I know that the message struck a chord with a number of people.

There are just some Moments that I write that I have such an emotional tie to. They make me wait with anticipation to hear the responses, to see if people "get it" like I did. I love the blend of the childhood sentiment with the power of God pursuing us.

This is a fitting message to end the book with, in that the message of the gospel is spoken here. To those who have already heard it and to those who have never quite come to grasp it.